Experiencing
Teacher Leadership

Experiencing Teacher Leadership

Perceptions and Insights from First-Year Teacher Leaders

Michael Coquyt

ROWMAN & LITTLEFIELD
Lanham • Boulder • New York • London

Published by Rowman & Littlefield
An imprint of The Rowman & Littlefield Publishing Group, Inc.
4501 Forbes Boulevard, Suite 200, Lanham, Maryland 20706
www.rowman.com

6 Tinworth Street, London SE11 5AL, United Kingdom

British Library Cataloguing in Publication Information Available

Library of Congress Cataloging-in-Publication Data Available

ISBN: 978-1-4758-4881-6 (cloth : alk. paper)
ISBN: 978-1-4758-4882-3 (pbk. : alk. paper)
ISBN: 978-1-4758-4883-0 (electronic)

∞™ The paper used in this publication meets the minimum requirements of American National Standard for Information Sciences—Permanence of Paper for Printed Library Materials, ANSI/NISO Z39.48-1992.

Contents

Foreword

"Tell me and I'll forget. Show me and I may remember. Involve me and I'll understand." This Chinese proverb resonates with Dr. Coquyt's vision of teacher leadership for both aspiring and seasoned leaders as they reflect on their progressive journey into leadership. His premise suggests that the more professionals are engaged in leadership roles, the more they will understand the benefits of change impacting teaching and learning. Concurrently, when school personnel value teacher leadership, trust and collaboration impact the potential to grow exponentially, ensuring that teachers' performance improves both in and outside the classroom. Ultimately, by creating opportunities to involve teacher leaders in supportive roles, school officials will be better prepared to support the professional growth of teachers, sustain the vision of the school, and impact student achievement.

Leadership development has traditionally focused on the administrator's responsibility for promoting and enhancing school improvement efforts. Today, there are a growing number of educators who believe that teacher leadership initiatives delivered by teachers for teachers plays a significant role in building a positive school culture. In *Experiencing Teacher Leadership: Perceptions and Insights from First-Year Teacher Leaders*, expert Michael Coquyt, EdD, offers a grassroots perspective for increasing the understanding of teacher leadership through a unique focus on actual teacher leaders in their first-year experiences on the job. This qualitative research investigation provides a seamless account of conversations with teacher leaders while remaining clearly focused on the voice of the teacher leader.

Based on the Teacher Leader Model Standards, this readable and insightful text journals pragmatic strategies for documenting the transition from classroom teacher to teacher leader. The book clearly describes the developmental phases that teachers experience during their transition to service as a leader. It illustrates how teachers can create change, grow as professionals, and become true leaders within their schools.

The book draws on the groundbreaking work of two previous texts, *The Leader Within: Understanding and Empowering Leaders* (2016) and *Growing Leaders Within: A Process toward Teacher Leadership* (2017), co-authored by Michael Coquyt and Brian Creasman. Coquyt's in-depth case study illustrates viable points that demonstrate how professional development supported by collaboration, teacher leadership, and andragogy/adult learning theory can be organized to share responsibilities with teachers, thereby instilling a genuine sense of pride and accomplishment.

Moreover, the book is a sincere outreach from Michael Coquyt, who advocates for the professional development of teachers willing to lead as empowered individuals. The book provides an important model of teacher leadership led by caring teacher leaders in partnership with the school and district-wide leaders. This text is a fascinating read for interested professionals who wish to explore teachers as leaders, leadership development, and progressive educational change.

John Frederick Ziegler, EdD
Professor, Educational Leadership Program
Edinboro University of Pennsylvania
Former School Administrator, 1987–2009

Preface

The writing of this book celebrates the culmination of three years of teaching, researching, and writing about the complexities of teacher leadership. Most books about teacher leadership, including one that was written with Dr. Brian Creasman in 2016, are written to explain what teacher leadership is and how it looks in schools throughout the nation. *The Leader Within* (2016) was written for that specific purpose.

Some books about teacher leadership are written with a particular audience in mind and examine teacher leadership through a particular lens. The second book, also written with Dr. Creasman, *Growing Leaders Within* (2017), was written specifically for administrators to assist in the meticulous task of identifying those teachers who have the disposition and temperament to become teacher leaders in their school or district. This book, *Experiencing Teacher Leadership*, takes a deep dive into the actual experiences of teacher leaders as they navigate their way through their first year on the job.

In order to genuinely understand some of the complexities of teacher leadership, it was important to find out for myself what the experiences of first-year teacher leaders was really like. This book chronicles the experiences of five novice teacher leaders in the months leading up to and including their first school year in a leadership position in their respective buildings.

Experiencing Teacher Leadership might be perceived as a companion to both *The Leader Within* and *Growing Leaders Within*. Well, it is and it isn't. References to *The Leader Within* are made numerous times in this book, and for good reason. In order to develop teacher leaders and grow a collaborative leadership culture, you need to know a thing or two about teacher leadership. In my humble opinion, *The Leader Within* is a good place to start. After acquiring knowledge about teacher leadership, the next logical measure is exercising that knowledge.

For a practicing administrator who wishes to identify, grow, and develop teacher leaders within his or her school or district, reading and analyzing *Growing Leaders Within* is a logical next step. *Growing Leaders Within* is different from previous works about teacher leadership due to its pragmatic nature, its use of the Teacher Leader Model Standards as a conceptual framework, and, maybe most important, the seven-step process of growing leadership capacity explained in the book is doable in today's educational settings.

The thing that sets *Growing Leaders Within* apart from most books about teacher leadership is the focus on professional development specifically for teacher leaders. If an administrator read *The Leader Within* and *Growing Leaders Within*, there would be no need to read this book. The process of taking novice teacher leaders through the seven stages of growth described in *Growing Leaders Within* adequately prepares them for the transition into teacher leadership.

Experiencing Teacher Leadership is unique from most other books about teacher leadership because the focus is on the teachers and their experiences, good and bad, as they transition from classroom teacher into a position of leadership in their school. For some this transition is seamless, while for some it is exacerbating to the point that they question why they entertained this thought in the first place. The hypothesis about the role change is quite simple: those who transition successfully into their new roles better understand the situation, themselves, the amount of support they need, and have knowledge of or have developed particular strategies to cope with this transition.

In very simple terms, is there a blueprint for those teacher leaders who experienced success? Can this blueprint or scheme be replicated so that others who are contemplating this transition can also find success? It is recommended that anyone considering a transition into a teacher leadership role should read this book first. No doubt some of the challenges the five teacher leaders in this book confronted will be universal for most first-year teacher leaders.

The reader may also find it helpful to examine the book in conjunction with where they are in their leadership journey. For example, chapter 2 examines the summer months preceding the beginning of the school year. It would be very beneficial for any new teacher leader to carefully read the preface, introduction, and chapters 1 and 2 during the summer to get an idea about what to expect and how to prepare for his or her new role as seen through the eyes of these five new teacher leaders. If there are a number of new teacher leaders beginning their journey together, could *Experiencing Teacher Leadership* be the focus of a book study that they all read collectively before and during the school year?

Some of the strategies and recommendations mentioned in the book came as a result of the research performed throughout the year. For example, the importance of keeping a personal journal was something that was discovered early on in the research. Only one of the five new teacher leaders kept a journal, but the positive impact it had on her experiences made too much sense not to include it in the book. Reading about this positive experience should motivate the reader to at least consider keeping a journal throughout his or her leadership experience.

The role of the administrator during this entire process can't be underestimated. The role of the administrator will be analyzed throughout this book, but suffice it to say that if the administrator shirks his or her responsibility of clearly defining responsibilities, expectations, and duties the teacher leaders will perform, the full potential of utilizing teacher leaders will not be realized. Of equal importance is the administrator sharing this vision with every teacher in his or her school well before the teacher leaders begin their work.

As stated in the introductory paragraph, this book is a culmination of years of teaching, writing (see books mentioned earlier), and researching teacher leadership. For the past four years, the university where I am employed, Minnesota State University, Moorhead, has offered a master's of science degree with an emphasis in teacher leadership. Although many of the enrolled students are not teacher leaders in the truest sense, they are asked repeatedly in many of these courses to reconsider their roles as only teachers and seek out leadership positions outside of their classrooms. Their written responses, online group discussions, and explanations about how these new endeavors align with the Teacher Leader Model Standards has provided an awareness of the types of leadership activities teachers are performing in schools and districts across the state.

The research used for this particular book utilized a multiple case study to understand the culture of teacher leadership and the challenges and successes of five first-year teacher leaders at schools in central, southern, and western Minnesota. The primary focus was on their experiences transitioning between the classroom and new teacher leadership position using Nancy Schlossberg's Transition Theory as a conceptual framework. Schlossberg's theory will be examined in greater detail later in the book.

Suffice it to say that according to Schlossberg, a positive transition depends on how individuals perceive their balance of resources to deficits in terms of the transition, their sense of competency, their sense of well-being, and their sense of health (Schlossberg, 1981, p. 7). In this book, it is argued that these are all aspects that must be considered by the teacher leader prior to his or her decision to change roles.

Choosing to leave the classroom and move into a leadership position is a difficult decision for many teachers. Much too often, school districts which have received funding to be used for instructional coaches choose the most veteran teachers or the current chair of one of the curricular departments to fill these positions. In some cases, little thought is given to exactly what it is these newly appointed leaders will actually be doing, what their responsibilities will be, and, most importantly, what criteria will be used to inform both the administrator and the new teacher leader that they are doing a quality job.

Experiencing Teacher Leadership provides numerous examples of things to consider for both the emerging teacher leader and the administrator alike. The examples and experiences examined in the book are real and should be beneficial to any teachers considering the move into a leadership position in their school.

This section of the book concludes with a simple exercise called you should read this book if

- you will be spending some of your time in a teacher leadership position at your school;
- you would like to know more about teacher leadership;
- administration has created a position for you and there isn't a clear definition of exactly what it is that you will be doing;
- you are interested in learning the successes and challenges of first-year teacher leaders;
- you are wondering if there are things that you should be doing to prepare yourself for your new role as a teacher leader; and/or
- you would like to know more about adult learning theory and how working with adults is different from working with children or students.

Acknowledgments

I want to recognize and applaud the work that teacher leaders do each day to make our schools the best for students. Schools today are complex organizations, and your dedication to the field of education is truly inspiring. Teaching future leaders remains the noblest profession that exists in today's society. Without teachers, specifically those who have left the classroom to assume leadership positions, I would not be able to write this book and I thank you for serving and leading.

It takes great courage to leave a secure and, for the most part, predictable position for one that in many cases is just the opposite. These five novice teacher leaders were leaving behind teaching positions that they had nurtured and developed for years. All of them were so accomplished in their roles as classroom teachers that it may seem inexplicable that they would want to transition into a role that was completely unknown and mysterious. Some wanted a change, some needed a change, and others wanted to test their leadership abilities. The one common denominator was that they all wanted to do something for the "greater good."

All of the novice teacher leaders, at one time or another, came to the understanding that in order to have the greatest impact on teaching and learning, they needed to leave their individual classrooms behind. Some who have had similar epiphanies were lured toward an administrative role. Dr. Brian Creasman and I argue in our book *The Leader Within* that today's school administrators are burdened with almost impossible responsibilities and that they are left to lead though lacking in time and resources. Many would argue that teachers are the greatest resource administrators have at their disposal. I would argue that the dedicated group of teacher leaders have eclipsed their classroom brethren in this regard.

Teacher leaders are different. As stated previously, they are courageous. In this book it is reasoned that they are innovative, assertive, resilient, and understand that working with adults is a lot different than working with students. The reader will also come to realize that teacher leaders prefer to lead from behind and enjoy the challenge of connecting the dots for their colleagues in a mentor or coaching relationship. Teacher leaders value the behind-the-scenes work that creates an effective school environment for students and the teachers they work with.

I am grateful for the support, help, and assistance of many people. First, I would like to thank the five teachers who participated in this research study who provided the basis for this book. Their contributions have been invaluable and will help others who begin the process of transitioning from the classroom to a leadership position at their school. I have been fortunate to work with a phenomenal and talented editorial and production team at Rowman & Littlefield for a third time. Tom Koerner has become a type of mentor for me and continues to believe in the importance of spreading the word about the value of teacher leadership in today's schools. I also want to thank Emily Tuttle, who has helped me to navigate the publishing process (again) and continues to provide invaluable feedback to make this book better.

A special thanks goes out to Dr. John Ziegler, who wrote the ideal foreword to *Experiencing Teacher Leadership*. His expertise in the area of teacher leadership continues to grow internationally as evidenced in his most recent work with China's Ministry of Education in Beijing to introduce selected teachers to the concept of teacher leadership. I am fortunate to call him a colleague. In addition, I want to thank my colleagues who reviewed my manuscript early on. I am fortunate and honored to have the support and endorsements from Dr. David Tack, Dr. David Kupferman, and Dr. Corey Steiner.

Most importantly, I am tremendously grateful to my family, especially my wife Brenda, for supporting, encouraging, and inspiring me to continue to write about teacher leadership. They, more than anyone else, have come to understand how important this subject is to me. I thank them in advance as I continue to explore and research a topic that has become a major part of my professional life over the past several years.

Introduction

It seems fitting here in the introduction to advance my description of teacher leadership. Teacher leadership might, and often does, look different from one school to another. Fortunately, there are some common characteristics or dispositions that all teacher leaders possess. Perhaps the best part about this short section is the notion that this undertaking or idea to grow teacher leadership in your school or district can start with you. In no particular order . . .

Teacher Leaders Have Initiative—Teacher leaders do not wait for permission to do what they know is good for their school and their students. Teacher leaders do not need administrative directives to know and understand what their school, their colleagues, and their students require to be successful. Having initiative is not enough. Teacher leaders are also creative, resourceful, and good planners. Take a minute to think about some needs and issues that currently exist at your school. How can you and a group of like-minded teachers take the initiative to come up with some creative solutions to these issues?

Teacher Leaders Are Assertive—A big part of being assertive is having confidence that your motives and goals are attainable. This confidence might come from prior achievements or quite possibly this is the first time you have been passionate enough about something that you have decided to "put yourself out there," so to speak. Having a good working knowledge of the bureaucracy of your school's organization will serve you well here. Assertive teacher leaders have also proven themselves to be respectful, sincere, and emotionally stable in their past dealings with colleagues and administration.

Teacher Leaders Are Invested—For the most part, teacher leaders have demonstrated their proficiency and competence as classroom teachers to their colleagues and the administration. After all, it is difficult to take on more responsibilities if you are not capable of doing the job that you were hired to do in the first place, which is to teach. In my experience, most teacher leaders have at least three years of classroom teaching experience under their belts. In order to calm the waters with classroom teachers, teacher leaders should remain in their classrooms for a portion of the day as well.

A portion of chapter 2 examines the relationships you once had with your colleagues and how this will change once you move into any type of leadership position at your school. If your colleagues see you as too different, it will be more difficult for you to establish a trusting relationship with them.

Teacher Leaders Understand Adult Learning Theory—Teacher leaders work primarily with their adult colleagues, and any experiences you might have had working with them on committees or a particular task force in the past will serve you well. Depending on what it is that you are asked to do in your new role, you might be setting expectations for your colleagues, asking them to complete certain tasks in a timely manner, and having them demonstrate to you that they understand and can apply certain topics that you have discussed with them.

Sounds a lot like teaching, right? Not quite. Think for a minute about how an adult might react to being asked to meet various expectations, complete certain tasks on time, and demonstrate their understanding of a topic. How is this different from how your students might respond?

A full list of teacher leader dispositions that have been established by prior researchers is provided in chapter 1. In my humble opinion, if a teacher leader has the initiative, is assertive, invests him- or herself fully in your school, and has successfully worked with colleagues in the past, he or she has the tools necessary to assume some type of leadership position at the school if he or she chooses to do so.

For some, like all of the teachers who took part in this research study, your building administrator might have already approached you about this possibility. If you are at this juncture, it would be nice to know what it is you are getting yourself into. The path toward leadership will not be the same for everyone as each individual, situation, and school is distinct. One thing that is indisputable is that the transition and your new role will be different from what you have experienced before.

Teachers who transition from the classroom into a position of leadership face many challenges. Some teachers are better equipped to cope with these challenges than others. Probably the most challenging aspect is moving into a position of leadership that for many is different from their role as a classroom teacher. "While presented as a catalyst for educational improvement, it blurs the traditional division between teaching and leading and therefore challenges the conventional professional relationships in schools as well as the professional self-understanding of teacher leaders" (Struyve, Meredith, & Gielen, 2014, p. 203).

Struyve, Meredith, and Gielen (2014) also noted, "The complexity of teacher leadership should be acknowledged and further unraveled, using empirical studies that help us to obtain a deepened understanding of the phenomenon of teacher leadership from an 'inner' perspective" (p. 208). My hope is that this book provides that insider or "inner" perspective after spending a year following and interviewing five new teacher leaders as they navigate their new positions. Individuals adapt to change differently (Schlossberg, 1981). Understanding the expectations and responsibilities that this new leadership position entails is also beneficial for the novice teacher leader and the teachers he or she will be working with as well.

As stated in the preface, a qualitative case study approach was used to illustrate the intricacies of not only the transition from the classroom but also practices the administration, and the aspiring teacher leader, can use to make this transition as seamless as possible. A case study approach seemed appropriate because the individuals', novice teacher leaders, in this case, perception of the transition is more important than the actual transition (Schlossberg, 1981, p. 5).

A case study can inform some of the specific factors that emerge that either hindered the transition or assisted in the transition from classroom teacher to teacher leader. It can also take into account ways of overcoming encumbrances that keep teacher leaders from doing what most were hired to do: work effectively with other teachers.

Five first-year teacher leaders participated in this study. It was truly fortunate to find a nice mix of schools, (high, middle, and elementary) for the study. A short description of each is provided below. All of the teacher leaders taught in a Midwestern school in the United States and all but one were to serve as instructional coaches for their building.

Teacher Leader A—She has spent twenty-plus years working as a high school (grades 9 through 12) teacher in a mid-sized school. She has been the chair of her department in the past and will oversee ten to fifteen teachers in her building. Her primary position is to serve as an instructional coach.

Teacher Leader B—She has spent twenty-plus years working at the same mid-sized high school as teacher leader A. She has been the chair of her department in the past and will oversee ten to fifteen teachers in her building. Her primary position is to serve as an instructional coach.

Teacher Leader C—She has spent seventeen years working at a mid-sized middle school (grades 5 through 8). Her central function is to serve as an instructional coach for roughly twenty to twenty-five teachers in her building.

Teacher Leader D—He has spent sixteen years in a mid-sized middle school. He brings seven years of head coaching experience to the position and will serve as an instructional coach for approximately twenty teachers.

Teacher Leader E—She has spent fifteen years teaching in a large elementary (kindergarten through grade 3) school. Her central task will be to coordinate the professional development activities and communicate with roughly sixty kindergarten teachers in sixteen different elementary schools.

Throughout the book, references will be made about teacher leader A (TLA) or teacher leaders B through E merely to provide a perspective for the reader. There will not be a detailed comparison among teacher leaders who participated in this study nor an assessment among grade levels. As stated earlier, it was fortunate to secure new teacher leaders from the three different levels (high, middle, elementary) and it was interesting to examine the perspective of the transition as seen through the eyes of a primary level teacher leader compared to that of a high school teacher leader.

The only factors that differentiate the new teacher leaders were the school level, previous leadership experiences, and role. Most teacher leaders found themselves serving as instructional coaches and this was anticipated. The only outlier was teacher leader E, whose role required her to work with a very large number of teachers from various schools within her district and her duties were quite different from those who served primarily as instructional coaches.

Although this book draws on a teacher leader perspective, it has the potential to contribute to and complement an administrative perspective in important ways for principals, superintendents, and others working in an educational setting. This book provides an understanding into what *new* teacher leaders do, the challenges they face, and the support systems they may or may not have. Ideally, this book would be read during the summer months preceding the beginning of the new school year. As readers will soon realize, the summer months constitute the Moving In stage of their new leadership journey.

HOW THE BOOK IS ORGANIZED

Much like *The Leader Within* and *Growing Leaders Within*, the goal of this book was to remain simple to read, understand, and use. Though educators will be the primary users of the book, it was important not to include what is referred to as "educational jargon" but instead offer clear and pragmatic strategies for explaining the transition from classroom teacher to teacher leader. This pragmatism is exemplified by the many "Self-Reflection" segments sprinkled throughout each of the chapters.

Just because the "Self-Reflection" segments are sprinkled does not mean that they are unimportant. Quite the contrary—they are of the utmost importance. One of the ideas set forth at the end of this chapter is the importance of journaling for anyone who finds him- or herself transitioning into a new role. Although the "Key Takeaways and Recommendations" portion of each chapter contains elements that merit contemplation, it is the ideas set forth by the "Self-Reflection" segments that should be included in the teacher leader's personal journal. It can't be stressed enough how important it is to set a little bit of time aside each day to jot down personal thoughts, reflections, and future plans in your personal journal.

The book is simple in organization and presentation. Each chapter, except for chapters 1 and 6, will follow this sequence:

1. Introduction
2. Pulse Check
3. Research Questions and Explanation of Findings
4. Key Takeaways and Recommendations
5. Chapter Summary

There is some terminology that will be used throughout this book. The three phases (Moving In, Moving Through, and Moving Out) appropriately describe the phases or stages that new teacher leaders pass through during their transition from classroom teacher to teacher leader position. These phases, explained in greater detail in chapter 1, in turn will be mentioned in the title of some of the chapters.

The Four Ss will also be used repeatedly throughout each chapter. The Four Ss are, in no particular order, *Situation*, *Supports*, *Self*, and *Strategies*. These four elements are essential to understanding transition theory. Each of these elements and how each relate to transition theory will be examined in greater detail in chapter 1.

Chapter 1 sets the stage for the reader by illustrating such things as teacher leadership, transition theory, and the Teacher Leader Model Standards. Chapter 2 will examine the Moving In phase for each of the teacher leaders. The timeframe for Moving In was defined as the summer months and the first two weeks of the new school year. The research questions, observations, and interviews conducted during this stage focused primarily on only one of the Four Ss—Situation. Interviews for this phase were conducted during week three of the new school year in September.

Chapters 3 and 4 examine the Moving Through phase. The timeframe for Moving Through was defined as the third week of school until right after the Christmas holiday break or early January. The research conducted during this stage focuses on all of the Ss—Situation, Self, Support, and Strategies. Two interviews were conducted during this stage. The first was conducted in late October and the second was conducted in late January, early February.

Chapter 5 assesses the Moving Out phase. The timeframe for the Moving Out phase was late January, early February until late May.

The table in appendix A on page 93 provides a visual of each interview, which of the Four Ss is examined, and when the interview took place. Chapter 6 will deliberate some final thoughts on the specific leadership experiences of the five teacher leaders and offer some recommendations for future teacher leaders to consider.

For the purposes of this research and the writing of this book, it was crucial to examine as many factors as possible during the "lived" experience. For example, the second S, see table 0.1, is an examination of Self. In this factor

Table 0.1.   Four Ss Summary and Factors

Situation
New Role
Positive or Negative?
Gradual or Sudden?
Internal or External?
Gain or Loss?
Duration
Colleagues—Impression*
Knowledge of Teacher Leadership*

Self
Strengths/Weaknesses
Control
Resiliency
Options
Stage of Life
Previous Experience—Adaptability

Support
Spouse/Partner/Family
Workspace—Physical Setting
Co-Workers
Institutional and Other Organizations

Strategies
Psycho—Self-Esteem/Personal Worth
Optimistic—Hope
Cope Well in Different Settings
Goal Setting
Planning
Health
Manage Emotions and Stress
Change View of Situation/Flexibility

*These elements were added for the purposes of this research.

a person is to consider his or her perceived strengths and weaknesses, *resiliency*, options, and *adaptability*. It is one thing to do this analysis before the actual experience but quite another to do the analysis when experiencing the phenomenon. For example, I was not as interested in the subject's perceived *resiliency* and *adaptability* before beginning his or her new position as I was in how resilient and adaptable he or she became while in his or her new role as a teacher leader.

PULSE CHECK

Quality teachers practice the art of self-reflection as a means to grow professionally. This portion of each chapter provides readers a place to record their thoughts as they begin their journey through each chapter. As mentioned previously, various "Self-Reflection" sections will be provided throughout each chapter. Some of these questions will compel readers to consider aspects of their journey that haven't yet been examined. This section provides a means to make segments in each chapter relevant to each individual's setting, experiences, and professional growth. It is also recommended that these thoughts be included in readers' personal journals.

RESEARCH QUESTIONS AND EXPLANATION OF FINDINGS

In this section of each chapter the questions that guided the research are disclosed. My journey toward understanding the transition from classroom teacher to teacher leader is much like anyone else who has researched a particular topic. There were questions about this transition that needed to be answered and examined at a deeper level.

The findings would in turn inform my understanding of teacher leadership in general, and a process to assist other teacher leaders during this transition in particular. The explanations of findings portion is just that: an explanation. Included in this section are numerous excerpts and quotes from the participants in an effort to bring the reader as close to the "lived" experience as possible.

Anyone who has performed research can appreciate the emotions one goes through when analyzing the results. A summary is provided below and each was experienced to some degree or another during this journey.

Pleased—Pleased and content when the findings affirmed that research that came before mine.

Excited—Excitement was felt when the research offered a new insight into the research and development of teacher leaders.

Confused—Anyone who has performed qualitative research understands this emotion. Countless hours were spent looking at some of the data that still had me questioning, "What exactly does this mean?"

Contemplative—Having researched and written two books about teacher leadership and presently teaching graduate level courses about teacher leadership, it is hard to not have preconceived notions about the topic being examined. Some of what was discovered forced me to reconsider what I thought I knew about teacher leadership and offered new insights into future inquiry.

KEY TAKEAWAYS AND RECOMMENDATIONS

This portion of each chapter is related to the "Pulse Check" segment studied earlier. Key takeaways are components that each aspiring teacher leader must understand in order to grow and develop as a true leader in his building or district. Additionally, this section allows the reader to identify his own key takeaways from each phase. This is a way to reflect on your learning in order to grow and transform as a teacher leader.

The "Recommendations" portion of the chapter can be used as a checklist for the new teacher leader. The concepts or ideas listed in this section characterize each phase. Special care was given to detailing some of the challenges teacher leaders face as they relate to the current phase. It should be noted that some of what is suggested in this section did not come from the research. Instead, various recommendations were the result of analyzing where the teacher leaders were mentally and emotionally and a solution was developed. An example of this can be found in chapter 4 when the Teacher Leader Plan and Teacher Leader Report are described.

CHAPTER SUMMARY

This section, obviously, comes at the end of each chapter. This section provides a clear, concise summary of most of the topics found within the phase and indicators pertaining to the growth of teacher leadership. The summary also offers an opportunity to plant seeds for future analysis. Here is the first seed: goal setting and evaluation.

One topic that will be revisited many times throughout this book is goal setting. Specifically, what is it that you wish to accomplish, how will you know you accomplished each goal, and how will you know or (measure) the effectiveness of each goal? Beyond goal setting is evaluation. How will you or your administrator measure proficiency? A suggestion is offered here and it will be examined in greater detail in chapter 4.

In chapter 4 the Professional Development Plan and Professional Development Report process is examined. This process is used in some higher education institutions to evaluate the effectiveness of a professor's work performance associated with five specific criteria. My suggestion is that this same process could be emulated using the seven domains contained in the Teacher Leader Model Standards as the criteria. Instead of using the words Professional Development, Teacher Leadership is substituted, producing the Teacher Leadership Plan (TLP) and Teacher Leadership Report (TLR). A list of the standards are given here for those unfamiliar with them.

Domain 1: Fostering a collaborative culture to support educator development and student learning.

Domain 2: Accessing and using research to improve practice and student learning.

Domain 3: Promoting professional learning for continuous improvement.

Domain 4: Facilitating improvements in instruction and student learning.

Domain 5: Promoting the use of assessments and data for school and district improvement.

Domain 6: Improving outreach and collaboration with families and community.

Domain 7: Advocating for student learning and profession.

Think of this portion of the introduction as "food for thought." Evaluation is probably not too high on your list of priorities at this stage of the game, but it is important to plant this seed. If done right, it can prove to be an invaluable resource as you navigate your first year in your new position. Page forward to the "Key Takeaways" section of chapter 4 to learn more about this detailed yet easy to understand process. A sample for Domain 1 is provided. A conversation about the TLP and evaluations might be a good topic for your pre-school-year meeting with your administration.

Self-Reflection

- Of the seven domains, which are most closely aligned to your new teacher leader role? Jot down a few activities that you know you will be performing that could fall under the domains on your list. How will you demonstrate that you have successfully met the criteria defined by the domain.
- What are some resources available to you that can assist with your efforts to keep an accurate journal of your daily activities? How important has journaling been in your previous role(s)?

Chapter 1

Setting the Stage

At first blush, the transition from classroom teacher to a position of leadership in your school might seem, to some, seamless and smooth. To others, this transition might be fraught with uncertainty. People who fall into the former have been, in my experience, former department chairs or head coaches. For this group of people, leadership has been an integral part of what they have been doing at their school for years. For those who have no previous leadership experience, the transition might be a little more challenging. The next section is designed not only for teacher leaders but for anyone who is experiencing transition in their current position.

My personal experiences with this type of transition occurred when I transitioned from classroom teacher to full-time graduate student/assistant, from high school teacher to district principal/superintendent, and traditional instructor to fully online instructor in higher education. Full disclosure, I had no knowledge of Schlossberg's theory or the Four Ss and their related factors during any of these transitions. But I can remember thinking long and hard about the situation I was moving into, whether it would benefit me and my family, the type of strategies I had to assist in the transition, and what kinds of supports I had at my disposal.

The Four Ss will be examined in greater detail shortly and the reader is allowed to take a deep dive into a couple of them by completing a few reflective exercises. Reflecting on the Four Ss will serve anyone well who is experiencing a transition in their lives.

At the end of this chapter you should become more familiar with the following:

- Schlossberg's Transition Theory as seen through the teacher leadership lens;
- the Four Ss: Situation, Self, Support, and Strategy; and the term "taking stock";
- the phases *Moving In, Moving Through, and Moving Out* and how they can be applied to transitioning into a new position;
- the Teacher Leader Model Standards; and
- the dispositions of teacher leaders.

TRANSITION THEORY

As stated in the preface, Schlossberg's Transition Theory will be used as the theoretical framework for the research portion of this book. Schlossberg's theory helps facilitate an understanding of adults in transition and directs them to the help they need to handle the "ordinary and extraordinary process of living" (Evans, et al., 2010, p. 213). According to Goodman, Schlossberg, and Anderson (2006), a transition is "any event or non-event that results in changed relationships, routines, assumptions, and roles" (p. 33). All four changes (relationships, routines, assumptions, roles) were experienced to one degree or another by teacher leaders transitioning from the classroom to their new leadership positions.

Schlossberg's theory also describes three different types of transitions. These are anticipated, unanticipated, and nonevents. Anticipated transitions happen expectedly. Assuming a leadership role for the upcoming school year was an expected transition. Unanticipated transitions happen unexpectedly and are not scheduled. Put into the context of this topic, this type of transition often occurs when the nuances of what the new leadership position entails become known. Nonevent transitions are those that an individual expected to occur but that did not happen. Administrative vision (or lack thereof) and having clear expectations for the new teacher leaders falls under this category.

The central issue during the transition period is adaptation—"how individuals adapt to a transition depends on how they perceive their balance of resources to deficits in terms of the transition, their sense of competency, well-being, and health" (Schlossberg, 1981, p. 7). How individuals adapt to a transition depends on how they perceive their balance of resources to deficits in terms of the transition, their sense of competency, their sense of well-being, and their sense of health (Schlossberg, 1981, p. 7). These factors affecting adaptation are of utmost importance and will be investigated at great length in subsequent chapters.

MOVING IN, MOVING THROUGH, MOVING OUT

A transition is actually a process that extends over time (Goodman, Schlossberg, & Anderson, 2006). At first people are consumed by their new role. Gradually, they begin to separate from the past and, as stated previously, establish new roles, relationships, routines, and assumptions. Transitions may provide opportunities for growth as well as decline. It is safe to state that all of the teachers who participated in this research grew as professionals and as leaders. Another assumption that will be examined in subsequent chapters is that the growth that the teacher leaders experienced resulted from their own initiative and drive to be proficient in their new roles.

Goodman, Schlossberg, and Anderson (2006) endorsed the idea of transitions having three phases, which they called Moving In, Moving Through, and Moving Out. People moving into a situation need to familiarize themselves with the rules, norms, and expectations of the new system.

Moving In (Komives & Brown, n.d.; Schlossberg, Waters, & Goodman, 1995) involves leaving a known context behind and entering a new context. Once in a new situation, individuals must learn to balance their activities with other areas of their lives as they move through the transition. Almost all of the participants in this research stated that they knew next to nothing about their new positions. All they knew was that they would be working with teachers in their subject areas and that they would no longer be teaching in their classrooms.

Self-Reflection

- Knowing what you do about your new position, list as many rules, norms, and expectations as you can on the Moving In table (table 1.1).

In the *Moving Through* phase, people begin the process of adjustment and day-to-day management (Komives & Brown, n.d.; Schlossberg, Waters, & Goodman, 1995). For the purposes of this book and the research conducted, this phase spanned from the third week of the school year just after the holiday break and the New Year. There was no science or mathematical calculations involved in determining how long the time between *Moving In* and *Moving Through* should be. In my experience (eleven years classroom

Table 1.1.   Moving In

Rules	•
	•
	•
Norms	•
	•
	•
Expectations	•
	•
	•

plus twelve years administration in PK–12), if you don't have things figured out after the first four months of the school year, you may never figure them out. Thankfully, all five new teacher leaders survived during the *Moving Through* phase.

Moving Out can be seen as ending one transition and thinking about what comes next. The *Moving Out* phase spanned from roughly late January, early February until late April, early May. It should be stated here that this stage does not mean transitioning to a new role or position but rather moving away from this position being so new and uncertain. It was during this phase when I asked the teachers to reflect on some of the most significant aspects and facets of their journey using the Four Ss as a backdrop. The research (primarily interviews and observations) that was conducted for the writing of this book follows the five new teacher leaders as they transition through each phase mentioned previously.

FOUR SS

Schlossberg's Transition Theory is based on the "Four Ss"—a system designed to assist individuals in understanding change. This system is often referred to as "taking stock" (Chickering & Schlossberg, 1995, p. 49; Evans, Forney, & Guido-DiBrito, 1998, p. 111). Table 1.2 lists each of the Four Ss. Before moving forward it is important to pump the brakes a little and look at the big picture for a moment. For this research, Goodman's phases (explained previously) were used in conjunction with the Four Ss. The table in appendix A on page 93 provides a visual for how the Four Ss (situation, support, self, and strategies) are related to each transition period (*Moving In, Moving Through,* and *Moving Out*).

Table 1.2. Transition Theory: Four Ss

Situation
Supports
Self
Strategies

A quick analysis of the table should make clear to the reader that not all of the factors are associated or correlate with each of Goodman's three phases. For example, it is next to impossible to investigate whether a transition is positive/negative or seen as a gain/loss during the *Moving In* phase. This examination about whether the transition was a positive or negative move is better situated in the *Moving Through* stage after the teacher leader has a few months on the job. Please take some time to examine the table in appendix A on page 93 before reading further.

The taking stock process involves determining an individual's resources— that is, "your situation, your supports, self, and your strategies" (Chickering & Schlossberg, 1995, p. 49). The factors related to each S are very important because not all teachers are going to cope with the transition in a similar fashion. For example, analyzing Situation involves an analysis of the new role, whether it was perceived as a positive or negative move, whether it was perceived as gradual or sudden, whether the decision to enter the new role was internal or external, whether it was perceived as a gain or a loss, and what was the duration? No two people will have the same experiences during the transition period.

Situation (as described by Chickering & Schlossberg, 1995, p. 51; Sargent & Schlossberg, 1988, p. 60) refers to how an individual interprets the transition. Does the individual perceive the transition as positive, negative, expected, unexpected, desired, or dreaded? Coping with Situation will vary according to what triggered the transition. Interestingly, there are some elements of the situation that the individual has control over and some he or she does not. For the purposes of this book, elements of situation the five teacher leaders had control over were the timing and previous experience with a similar transition.

Those elements where little control was exercised included the new roles the individual was taking on and the duration of the transition. Aspects of Situation examined in this book included the new role itself, whether it was viewed as a positive or negative move, whether it was gradual or sudden, whether it was internal (choice made by individual) or external (choice made by someone else), whether the situation was perceived as a gain or a loss, and the duration. A summary of Situation is provided in table 1.3.

Table 1.3.   Situation

New Role
Positive or Negative?
Gradual or Sudden?
Internal or External?
Gain or Loss?
Duration
Knowledge of Teacher Leadership
Colleagues

$\underline{S}$elf (as described by Chickering & Schlossberg, 1995, p. 60; Sargent & Schlossberg, 1988, p. 60) defines what type of strengths and weaknesses the individual brings to the transition. Previous experience definitely has a role in this S. From this research it can be determined that what is central in $\underline{S}$elf is control, resiliency, and perceived options. This is probably the most important of the Four Ss and it deserves a little more attention than some of the others. Table 1.4 summarizes the factors associated with $\underline{S}$elf. Please perform the self-reflection activity provided in table 1.5 before moving on to $\underline{S}$upport.

Self-Reflection

• An analysis of $\underline{S}$elf, similar to the exercise shown in table 1.5, should be done by anyone, not only teacher leaders prior to even contemplating a transition into a new role. There is a reflective portion for each element. Please take note that not all elements of $\underline{S}$elf are listed.

$\underline{S}$upport (as described by Chickering & Schlossberg, 1995, p. 55; Sargent & Schlossberg, 1988, p. 60) reveals sources of support available to the person in transition. Support could be from a spouse or partner, family member(s), friend(s), co-worker(s), neighbor(s), organization(s), or

Table 1.4.   Self

Strengths/Weaknesses
Control
Resiliency
Options
Stage of Life
Previous Experience—Adaptability
Health
Changed View of Situation/Adaptability

Table 1.5. Rating Self

Think About and Rate the Following Factors Associated with Self			
How much **control** do you need in a typical situation in order to be comfortable?	4 None	3 Very Little	2 Some	1 Ultimate

Knowing what you do about your new role, how much control will you be given to perform day-to-day operations and make key decisions? How does this match with your rating?

When faced with uncertainty or doubt in the past, how would you rate your ability to find **options** or **alternatives** that most people in your group or organization were happy with?	4 Exemplary	3 Accomplished	2 Developing	1 Beginning

Based on what you know about your new position, how might you need to utilize these factors?

When faced with uncertainty or doubt in the past, how would you rate your ability to **adapt** and develop a different understanding of the situation?	4 Exemplary	3 Very Well	2 Developing	1 Inconsistent

Based on what you know about your new position, what are some ways it is different from what you have done in the past?

Table 1.6.   Support

Spouse/Partner/Family
Workspace—Physical Setting
Co-Workers
Institutional and Other Organizations

Table 1.7.   Strategies

Self-Esteem/Personal Worth
Optimistic—Hope
Cope Well with Different Settings
Goal Setting
Planning
Health
Manage Emotions and Stress
Change View of Situation/Flexibility

institution(s). (See table 1.6.) Sources of support can be both positive and negative. Having a satisfying workspace and physical setting is also important here. People receive support from family, friends, intimate relationships, and institutions and/or communities. The focus for this book was the support received by colleagues and the administration.

Strategies (as described by Chickering & Schlossberg, 1995, p. 66; Sargent & Schlossberg, 1988, p. 60) involve questions such as whether an individual uses more than one coping strategy, can the individual creatively cope by changing the way he or she views the situation, can the individual manage his or her emotions/reactions to the stress of the transition, and is the person flexible? Goodman, Schlossberg, and Anderson (2006) emphasized that individuals cope best when they remain flexible and use multiple strategies. Other aspects of Strategies examined in this book included optimism, goal setting, planning, and physical health. (See table 1.7.)

For the purpose of this research, second in importance to Self is Strategies. A similar self-reflection exercise that was performed for Self is provided in table 1.8. Please complete the activity prior to continuing on to the segment about teacher leadership.

TEACHER LEADERSHIP

Teacher leadership is a term that is not easily defined. As you will read in chapter 2, none of the five participants had a good working definition of what

Table 1.8.   Rating Strategies

Think About and Rate the Following Factors Associated with Strategies			
How much time and effort have been devoted to **goal setting and planning** in your current position?	4 Very Much	3 Considerable	2 Some	1 Very Little

Knowing what you do about your new role, how much control will you be given to set goals and develop and implement personal or individual plans? How does this match with your rating?

When faced with uncertainty or doubt in the past, how **resilient** and **flexible** have you been in your efforts to find a common ground or arrive at a satisfactory conclusion?	4 Exemplary	3 Accomplished	2 Developing	1 Beginning

Based on what you know about your new position, how might you need to utilize these factors?

When faced with uncertainty or doubt in the past, how have you managed your **emotions** and dealt with the **stress** that accompanied the situation?	4 Exemplary	3 Very Well	2 Developing	1 Inconsistent

Based on what you know about your new position, how much more stressful will it be compared to the stress and emotions faced when teaching?

teacher leadership is or could list some of the good work done by teacher leaders in schools today. Neumerski (2012) refers to it as an "umbrella term referring to a myriad of work" (p. 320). Teacher leaders can be working in schools as coordinators, instructional coaches, specialists, lead teachers, and mentor teachers (Mangin & Stoelinga, 2008).

Wenner and Campbell (2016) explain that it is this "muddiness" that makes the term both captivating and dangerous at the same time (p. 135). Since York-Barr and Duke (2004) published their seminal work concerning teacher leadership, a lot has changed. For instance, Teacher Leader Model Standards (Teacher Leadership Exploratory Consortium, 2012) have been created, and in January 2014 the national Teacher Leadership Initiative was formed. Additionally, university degree programs, certificates, and endorsements in teacher leadership seem to be on the rise.

Many research articles have previously been published about the characteristics or dispositions that teacher leaders must possess in order to be effective. A summary of these dispositions is listed in table 1.9.

Rosenholtz's (1989) and Wilson's (1993) research put forward that teacher leaders are innovative risk takers who inspire their colleagues to be problem solvers. The idea of teacher leaders as risk takers and quality teaching was mentioned in York-Barr and Duke's (2004) research. Crowther, Kaagan, Fer-

Table 1.9.   Teacher Leader Characteristics

Author(s), Date	Characteristic(s)
Collins, 2001	Humility
Kouzes & Posner, 2002	Credibility
Badarocco, 2002	Modesty
Allio, 2005	Character
	Creativity
	Compassion
York-Barr & Duke, 2004	Collaborative
	Dependable
	Supportive
	Knowledgeable
	Flexible
Crowther, Kaagan, Ferfuson, & Hann, 2002	Professional Image
	Trustworthy
Wilson, 1993	Hard Worker
	Innovative
	Motivational
	Dedicated
Coquyt & Creasman, 2017	Passionate
	Initiative

guson, and Hann (2002) conducted a five-year study of schools in Australia. This research identified characteristics regarding respect, growth mindset, and translating ideas into actions. Regarding empathy, Allio (2005) argues, "No leadership program even attempts to engender compassion on the part of its students, to infuse them with emotional intelligence, a concept that has been actively promoted in recent leadership initiatives" (p. 1073).

Choosing the right candidates to be teacher leaders is no small task. Administrators must be diligent and thorough to ensure that the right teachers are chosen to become teacher leaders. This brings up an interesting question. Is having the proper dispositions enough to ensure a successful transition into the role of teacher leader? My contention is that having the right dispositions isn't enough to guarantee success. How a teacher leader copes with and adapts to the transition is very important and that needs to be explored further.

Empirical studies of teacher leadership are rather rare (Muijs & Harris, 2006, 2007; Smylie, 1997). Moreover, Smylie (1995) posits an inconsistency between the increasing amount written about teacher leadership and the small proportion consisting of systematic empirical investigations and studies using formal theory to focus research questions and to develop new theoretical insights. My hope is that this research and the writing of this book will in some small measure help to fill this void.

TEACHER LEADER MODEL STANDARDS REVISITED

This book, similar to *The Leader Within* and *Growing Leaders Within*, utilizes the Teacher Leader Model Standards developed by the Teacher Leader Exploratory Consortium (2012) to provide a conceptual framework for the experienced and aspiring teacher leader. In today's education circles, the terms "teacher leader" and "teacher leadership" are growing, with many asking the question, "What is a teacher leader or what is teacher leadership?" By utilizing the Teacher Leader Model Standards, both teacher leader and teacher leadership become clearer, as well as more practical.

The Teacher Leader Model Standards were not created to be a detailed job description. In other words, neither teachers nor school administrators should utilize the Teacher Leader Model Standards to create job criteria; instead they are to be used as guiding practices for effective teacher leadership. The standards provide a blueprint for leadership opportunities. To review, the Teacher Leader Model Standards are divided into seven domains:

Domain 1: Fostering a collaborative culture to support educator development and student learning.

Domain 2:   Accessing and using research to improve practice
                and student learning.
Domain 3:   Promoting professional learning for continuous improvement.
Domain 4:   Facilitating improvements in instruction and student learning.
Domain 5:   Promoting the use of assessments and data for school
                and district improvement.
Domain 6:   Improving outreach and collaboration with families
                and community.
Domain 7:   Advocating for student learning and profession.

The domains are further expanded by a set of functions for each teacher leader to perform. A more in-depth analysis of these domains will be included in chapter 2. The Teacher Leader Model Standards provide experienced and aspiring teacher leaders guiding practices to utilize to strengthen practice as well as professional growth. The book *The Leader Within* was written in part to encourage professional growth by providing teachers practical understanding, strategies, guided questions, and self-reflection opportunities aligned to each of the Teacher Leader Model Standards domains and functions.

The Teacher Leader Model Standards provide a set of principles that assists in growing teacher leadership in schools and school districts. The Teacher Leader Model Standards encourage teacher leadership to be developed or grown by embedding in the school process instead of in isolation. In schools and school districts where teacher leadership already exists, the Teacher Leader Model Standards will assist in strengthening professional growth practices. The result of using the Teacher Leader Model Standards is continuous improvement and growth of teacher leaders, two principles that are conveyed throughout the domains and functions. Needless to say, any book written about teacher leadership without mention of the Teacher Leader Model Standards would be incomplete.

CHAPTER SUMMARY

The primary focus at the beginning of this chapter was to decipher not only a professional transition into a new role but specifically a transition that involves added leadership duties and responsibilities for new teacher leaders. It is imperative that the classroom teachers are informed by administration very early on that the teacher leaders who are assuming teacher leadership roles are not joining the administrative team.

Creasman and Coquyt (2016) describe the differences between educational leaders (superintendent, principal, vice principal) and teacher leaders by using the *Nine Characteristics of High-Performing Schools* in their book *The Leader Within*. The complete table can be found in appendix B on page 95. Although educational leadership and teacher leadership are different, they are interconnected. The authors assert:

> A culture of effective school leadership, where all leaders work toward the same goals, mission, and vision, empower stakeholders to focus on student achievement. The typical "turf wars" are nonexistent, as everyone understands their role in leading the school to become a high-performing organization. (xvi)

It is important for new teacher leaders to understand the culture of the school in which they work. If the school culture is progressive, open minded, and puts students first, the transition for new teacher leaders should be quite smooth. Classroom teachers will soon realize that teacher leaders are not administrators but are colleagues whose job it is to assist them, work alongside them, and support them in their efforts to improve as teaching professionals. If the school's culture is reactionary and very conservative, things might not go so smoothly.

The Four Ss (Situation, Self, Support, and Strategies) might be a new concept for most people. The activities and information provided in this chapter should be helpful for any individual who is contemplating a professional transition. Although Strategies and Self were examined in greater depth, Situation and Support should not be overlooked. It is sensible to begin with Strategies and Self because, as the reader will soon find out, the Situation may be vague and unclear and the Support nonexistent.

Self-Reflection—As explained earlier, the "Self-Reflection" questions should be put in your personal journal.

- Read through the *Nine Characteristics of High-Performing Schools* found in appendix B. Which school characteristic is most closely aligned to your new position? There could be more than one. Can you summarize how the role of an educational leader is different from your role as a teacher leader? Could you explain this difference to colleagues who ask about your new role?
- Come up with your personal definition of leadership. How can your new role allow you opportunities to exercise and experience leadership activities that match your definition?

Chapter 2

Moving In

Planning and Preparation

This chapter will examine the "Moving In" phase, characterized as the time period from summer months and including the first two weeks of the new school year. The first interview for the new teacher leaders took place at the end of the second week in their new roles. Most of the new teacher leaders who took part in this research knew very little about the skills teacher leaders need to have, most possessed limited knowledge about teacher leadership in general and were left to fend for themselves, for the most part, in their preparation for their new positions. That being said, the purpose of this chapter is to provide new teacher leaders with some valuable resources that will hopefully make the transition from classroom teacher to teacher leader as seamless as possible.

Was there ever a time of change in your life when you knew exactly what it was that you were getting yourself into? Some might argue that you never know exactly what you are up against when going through a change, but using the word "exactly" proposes significance. Knowing what you are up against implies that you have an understanding of what is to be expected. Knowing *exactly* causes one to pause and consider things other than your own beliefs.

Transitioning from classroom teacher to a teacher leadership position is considered a major change for almost every teacher leader I have spoken with over the past three years. My advice is don't assume anything and find out as early as possible what the duties and responsibilities are for your new position. The reason for this statement is because in my experience, sometimes the only thing that has been deliberated by administration is that what you will be doing at your school next will be different from what you did the past year.

At the end of this chapter you should be more familiar with and better prepared to resolve the following:

- Take ownership of your new role right from the beginning. <u>Empower yourself</u> by setting personal goals and sharing them with your administrator.
- Gain a <u>broad understanding of teacher leadership</u> by examining the Teacher Leader Model Standards. This will eventually lead to a narrower focus by identifying domains and functions specific to your new role.
- Your <u>relationship with your colleagues</u> will change.
- Develop a short <u>list of essential skills</u> you will need in your new role.

PULSE CHECK

This portion of each chapter provides the reader with an opportunity to revisit the Four Ss and determine how each factor is or is not related to each stage. I have provided a table that can be used as a reference for the "Moving In" stage. A similar table will be provided in each subsequent chapter. In chapter 2 only *Situation* will be examined and the reader no doubt noticed that not all of the factors are directly associated with "Moving In". For example, it is next to impossible to determine if the new Situation is positive or negative, considered a gain or a loss, or how long you will be staying in your new role during the "Moving In" stage. These questions will be considered in the next few chapters.

There are a few things to glean from the "Moving In" phase by analyzing the Situation table (2.1). My advice is to gain as much knowledge about exactly what it is that you will be doing in your new role as you can. Press your administration to explain in great detail what your new role entails, and if they can't answer your questions, chances are that they don't know themselves. This doesn't bode well for you, but if you are reading this book, it is a step in the right direction.

Table 2.1.   Situation

New Role
Positive or Negative?
Gradual or Sudden?
Internal or External?
Gain or Loss?
Duration
Knowledge of Teacher Leadership
Colleagues

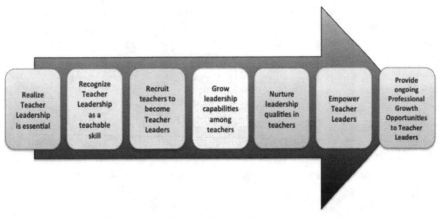

Figure 2.1. Seven Phases: Growing Teacher Leaders

In a perfect world, your administrator has followed the steps recommended in *Growing Leaders Within* and you have a pretty good idea what your new role will entail. A visual of the seven steps or phases used toward teacher leadership from *Growing Leaders Within* is provided in figure 2.1. Your journey from recruitment, through the growth and nurture phases, to where you are now has not only empowered you but has also offered you more than a glimpse at your new role. Unfortunately, this isn't always the case.

Chances are you were recruited by your administrator to perform this new role and nothing has been done to build a culture of teacher leadership at your school. On a more positive note, quite possibly your new role isn't new to your school at all and you are replacing or assisting a very successful teacher leader who has defined and refined the role over a number of years.

Self-Reflection

• Where does your new role fall in the scale in table 2.2? If your role is situated nearer to 1, what are some challenges and opportunities that this presents?

Table 2.2. Rate Your New Role

Established	Burgeoning	Very New
Respected	Gaining Respect	Unknown
Defined Duties/ Responsibilities	Evolving Duties/ Responsibilities	No Definite Duties/ Responsibilities
5	4	3	2	1

The other two factors from the Situation table that can be examined during the "Moving In" phase are gradual/sudden and internal/external. These factors are interrelated and almost need to be investigated together. For example, if a transition is sudden, there isn't much time to think about how motivated you are to make such a change or if you even want to do it at all. In my estimation there is no worse kind of change than one that is sudden and external (made by someone else).

On the opposite end of the spectrum is a gradual, internal transition. An internal transition is one that has been contemplated for quite some time. None of the five teachers who participated in this study stated that their transition was sudden. All of the teachers were given the summer months to gradually prepare themselves mentally and emotionally for their new roles as teacher leaders.

Some changes come about through a conscious decision by the individual (internal) and other changes are thrust upon the individual by other people or circumstances (external). Schlossberg hypothesized that a person adapts more easily if the change was a choice made by the individual (1981, p. 9). One aspect of this research that was very interesting but not surprising was that only one of the five teachers had true, internal motivation to leave the classroom. In other words, this decision was hers and not something that was put into her mind by the administration.

The other four teachers were approached by their principals and asked to contemplate the transition. It is unnecessary to spend a lot of time on this topic here, but if classroom teachers have no idea that leadership opportunities exist in their school or district, how would they be internally motivated to make such a change? It also begs the question, why is it that the only transition that is contemplated by most teachers, at least in my experience, is that from classroom teacher to administrator?

Self-Reflection

- How are leadership positions publicized in your school or district?
- How often is teacher leadership discussed in your school or district?

RESEARCH QUESTIONS AND
EXPLANATION OF FINDINGS

This portion of each chapter will examine some of the answers to the research questions that were asked of the five participants that contributed to this study. Of utmost importance, from the first interview, was finding out not only what each participant understood about teacher leadership but also how they were prepared or were being prepared for their new role in the upcoming school year.

Empowerment also needs to be mentioned in this section. Hypothetically, if someone reading this book were transitioning into a teacher leadership role in the fall of the next school year and there had been no training or professional development provided by administration, it would be helpful to have some type of framework from which to begin planning or at least have an idea about what to expect. It is hoped that this book in general and this chapter in particular will provide that framework.

Some common themes that emerged after an analysis of the data from the first interview were lack of training, a deficiency in understanding true teacher leadership, the importance of having a gradual transition period, intimate motivation, and a change in the relationships with their colleagues. These themes will be examined in greater detail here.

No Training

Central to the "Moving In" portion of the research study was how the teacher leaders perceived their new role with special attention given to the training they received over the summer and their knowledge about teacher leadership and adult learning theory. The results of the interviews were eye opening. No formal training was given to any of the teacher leaders I interviewed. TLA asserted, "Overall, I had no training other than what I put into it."

Some of those interviewed explained that they watched various podcasts about teacher leadership and instructional coaching and read a few books over the summer, but that was about it. TLB stated, "I would definitely say I wish I had more training. We are definitely learning as we go." TLD affirmed, "We have had to teach ourselves." Added to this frustration was a lack of vision from the administration. TLC indicated, "I don't think [the administrator] really knew what he wanted us to do." TLA explained it this way,

> I think that by giving us some latitude and not really having solid parameters and boundaries, we are able to figure out what works best in this position for this school for our departments and for the teachers we are working with. It is good, I think, but it feels weird.

Not everything that was discovered was negative. All of the teacher leaders stated that they planned to meet as a group once a month. All of those interviewed stated at the end of the study that this was the most beneficial aspect of not only their initial training but the program as a whole. Many interviewed explained that their understanding of what they are supposed to do is "evolving." TLE stated, "I look forward to going to those meetings just to learn. We have a safe place to share our frustrations."

Knowledge of Teacher Leadership

It was a little surprising that none of the participants had a good working knowledge of teacher leadership and the current work that teacher leaders do in school districts across the country. TLC defined teacher leadership: "It would be a teacher who takes the lead and I think I've always had it." The questions asked about the topic of teacher leadership elicited reflective responses about possible reasons why they were chosen by their administrators for their new role.

TLB asserted, "For the most part I get the job done in an effective manner that everyone can work with." Aside from reflecting on their past leadership accomplishments, it was satisfying to hear that most began thinking about how they plan to effectively work with their colleagues. When talking about building positive relations with their colleagues, TLA responded, "They are not going to want to play ball with me if they feel threatened or fearful."

Gradual or Sudden

Many transitions are expected and may be even inevitable or are a result of a deliberate decision (Schlossberg, 1981). Transitions that have a gradual onset are easier to adapt to because the individual can prepare for them (Schlossberg, 1981, p. 9). All of the participants indicated that the transition into their new role was gradual. All were approached by their administrators the year prior about the possibility of them leaving the classroom and assuming a new role as a teacher leader at the beginning of the 2017–2018 school year.

This is not to say that all of them jumped at the opportunity to change roles, and most actually wished to remain in their classrooms. A couple of them indicated that they struggled with the thought of leaving the classroom. TLE stated, "I wasn't interested in leaving my classroom. I told my principal that I wasn't done teaching." TLA acknowledged, "I struggled with that a little bit and questioned why my principal didn't want me to work with students any longer." TLB indicated, "Seriously, the brightest spot of my day is spending time with those kids. This was a struggle for me. . . . I really had to think things out." TLC reported to the contrary, "This is something I wanted to do . . . something that I was interested in."

Interestingly, the term "greater good" came up time and time again in the teachers' responses. The ability to impact more than just their classroom students is what ultimately made a few of the teachers decide that this is something that they wanted to pursue. TLD related a conversation he had with a veteran teacher leader that ultimately made him think that this would be a good move for him.

I told him that I was a little uneasy about leaving the classroom and he made the point that, look at it from this standpoint, you are passionate about helping kids in your classroom; think about how much more you can do by taking that passion and applying it to a larger mass of students. When I started to look at it from that vantage point, that is, when I seriously considered making the change. What I could do to help a larger mass of students . . . that is when I knew it was okay to transition into this new position.

Internal or External

Some changes come about through a conscious decision by the individual and other changes are thrust upon the individual by other people or circumstances (Schlossberg, 1981). Schlossberg hypothesizes that "the individual adapts more easily to transitions in which the source is internal" (p. 9). All of the teachers explained that the ultimate decision to pursue their new role was internal and most viewed this as something fresh and challenging. TLA posited, "I want to challenge myself to see if I can help others. There are a lot of things I think I do pretty well but this is new to me." TLB stated, "This is a new challenge. When you do something for sixteen years (taught sixth-grade math) I was looking for something a little different."

An interesting supplement that was uncovered in this segment was the focus on teamwork and creating more of a team mentality among their colleagues. This "team mentality" seemed to have its roots in their involvement in high functioning Professional Learning Centers (PLC) and a willingness to share with others what made these teams successful. TLD likened his new role to that of a bridge.

I think we are almost like a bridge to get teams to work together. If you have high functioning grade levels and they work well together, you can see that their kids are successful. Some teams work better together than others. I think our position is important to getting in there and knowing we need to collaborate together and bring some resources and strategies to them that can help.

Colleagues

This final area of investigation doesn't necessarily fit into any of the Four Ss, but it was one that I believe merited further examination. This area had to do with how the new teacher leaders were perceived by their colleagues and how (if at all) their relationships with them had changed during the summer and first few weeks of school. Oddly, for most of the teachers, their roles and responsibilities were not shared formally with their colleagues until the beginning of the school year during in-service.

There was some mention of them possibly doing something different at the end of the previous school year, but that was all the information shared by the administration with the rest of the staff. Most of their responses to questions about their relationships with their colleagues included words like "trust," "guarded," and "uncomfortable." This is to be expected. All their colleagues knew was that they would no longer be teaching but would instead be working with teachers and providing support for them in their classrooms. TLC put it this way, "We were thrown into this limbo-land where you're not a teacher, you're not one of us, but you're not an administrator either."

Almost all of the teacher leaders indicated that they would need to establish their colleagues' trust to allow them to do quality work, but none were sure how this would be accomplished. Most of them planned to have a one-on-one conversation with each of the teachers they were to work with, and for the most part this was accomplished during the first two weeks. It was during these meetings that other questions cropped up.

TLE commented, "They think I have some evaluative power or I want to evaluate them. I've said many times that this is not part of my job." TLC stated, "One today said that they think there is more going on." That same teacher reported that another colleague made the comment, "I hope she doesn't get me fired." Even if their colleagues didn't understand their new roles, these teachers, for the most part, did. TLA asserted,

> One thing that has changed is my role with them. My interactions have changed. I don't think it is a big mystery that we as teachers vent to each other all the time. That includes not only the students but also staff members. If we have a difficult situation with a colleague you go to a trusted person in the department and vent and that is the end of it. I can't do that anymore.

TLE summarized the first two weeks in her new role as follows:

> I always feel like someone is watching me . . . my behavior is being assessed at any given time. How I react, what I say, it's a leadership thing. People are looking to you and it changes your demeanor a little bit. Before, I could be one of the kids, now I have to be more of the grown-up . . . if that makes sense.

KEY TAKEAWAYS AND RECOMMENDATIONS

This portion of each chapter will be devoted to an examination of some of the key outcomes from each transition phase and a few recommendations gleaned from the experiences of the new teacher leaders as they moved through each phase. There were actually quite a few interesting elements realized after interviewing these five novice teacher leaders during the "Moving In" phase. The top two outcomes and the subject of much of the informal conversations between the teacher leaders and myself focused on the following:

What skills are associated with teacher leadership?
What exactly is teacher leadership?

In order to answer these very important questions, my advice would be to begin your deliberations and preparations as soon as possible. The questions and reflective exercises contained at the end of each of the following segments are a good first step toward your understanding of the skills you will need to be successful in your new teacher leader position. The skills associated with teacher leadership will be examined first. The last segment will focus on a deeper assessment of the Teacher Leader Model Standards. Taken together, both segments will better prepare the novice teacher leader for some of the challenges he or she faces when transitioning into his or her new role.

It is fair to conclude that in this research not a lot of thought was given by administration about exactly what each of the new teacher leaders would be doing in their new roles. Just because this was true in these situations does not mean that it is true for all new teacher leaders transitioning into a new role. A direct consequence of not knowing what they would be doing is a general lack of training for these new teacher leaders. It is hard to receive training for a position you know nothing about.

Even though the five teacher leaders received little to no training for their new positions, they did have a lot working in their favor. For example, all of them were previously employed as classroom teachers in the same district. This being said, all of them had a history with their schools and a good understanding of the culture, mission, and vision, and some of the curricular initiatives and programs. All of them also had good professional relationships with the teachers in their respective buildings, but none of them had any specific teacher leadership training.

Knapp (2017) stated, "It is presumptuous to think that teachers intuitively know how to lead their colleagues or schools without any focused support" (p. 251). Support in the form of some type of training should have occurred over the summer months. Some teacher leaders, as the reader will discover in subsequent chapters, did what they could to prepare by reading articles and finding resources about teacher leadership on the web. A good starting point for any training program should be an examination of the skills associated with most teacher leadership positions, and these skills are listed here.

Included in each skill are definitions and questions to consider as you prepare for your new position for the upcoming school year. Much of this information is taken directly from the book *Growing Leaders Within*, specifically chapter 7 and the Teacher Leader Model Standards. The important thing to remember is the context in which the skills will be applied. The novice teacher leader must contemplate, to the best of his or her ability, each skill in the context of being a teacher leader and not a classroom teacher. Many of these skills will be touched on in chapter 2 and reexamined in chapter 6 with an eye toward how each participant perceived him- or herself developing in his or her leadership skill capacity.

Communication

Communication is essential for all people in a leadership position. Previous research has proven, and the current research affirms, that teacher leaders often use face-to-face communication as the medium of choice to speak to classroom teachers, other teacher leaders, and stakeholders. In some cases, teacher leaders perform communication differently as they seek to use communication to engage diverse perspectives in the decision-making process.

Though teacher leaders utilize all available tools (such as social media and email) to communicate, this research suggests that they overwhelmingly prefer face-to-face communication. Teacher leaders understand how effective communication impacts relationships (Coquyt and Creasman, 2017, p. 95). Below, in table 2.3, are some questions and a rating scale about communication for you to examine as you prepare for your new teacher leader position.

1. What is your preferred mode of communication?
2. What are a few things you will need to do in order to develop this skill?

Table 2.3.   Communication Skills

Rate How Capable You Are with the Following Teacher Leader Skill (4) *Very Capable* (3) *Capable* (2) *Somewhat Capable* (1) *Not Capable at All*			
Communication 4	3	2	1

Based on what you know about your new position, how might you utilize this skill?

If this skill is considered a growth area (1 or 2), what can you do right now to improve your proficiency?

Organization

Organization is important for all leaders to grasp in order to be effective in their roles. On any given day, the teacher leader might be coaching and mentoring teachers, advocating in the local community for additional supports and resources for students, as well as supporting professional learning communities (Coquyt & Creasman, 2017, p. 97). According to Gehrke (1991), organizational skills help teachers to: 1) continue teaching and improving their own teaching; 2) monitor and evaluate current practices in the school; 3) coach and mentor others in developing effective curriculum and instructional practices; 4) engage in the decision-making process; 5) facilitate and lead professional learning for others; and 6) create a culture of collaboration. Questions to contemplate include:

1. How important is organization to teacher leaders? To leaders in general?
2. How would teachers characterize the need for the teacher leader to be organized?
3. How do the organizational skills needed for your new position compare to those employed in the classroom?

Table 2.4. Organization Skills

Rate How Capable You Are with the Following Teacher Leader Skill (4) *Very Capable* (3) *Capable* (2) *Somewhat Capable* (1) *Not Capable at All*			
Organization 4	3	2	1

Based on what you know about your new position, how might you utilize this skill?

If this skill is considered a growth area (1 or 2), what can you do right now to improve your proficiency?

Adult Learning Theory

Stated quite simply, working with adults is a lot different from working with students. Teaching adults is definitely different from teaching students and even dissimilar to working with them. Most teacher leaders have experience working with their colleagues before, so working with them now shouldn't be much different, or will it? Working together as colleagues is different from working with someone who is now seen as different, right or wrong. Barth (2013) warns of trying to make changes in a leveling profession:

Teachers are, in a way, their own worst enemy when it comes to unlocking leadership because they don't welcome it, typically don't respect it, and often feel threatened by one of their own taking it on. Anyone who bumps above the level is subject to condemnation: "Who the heck do you think you are?!" I'm not talking about trends—I'm talking about people impeding teacher leadership. Some of the people are called principals, and some are called teachers. (p. 10)

Barth's comments provide some food for thought. Here is some additional information for you to think about in regard to Adult Learning Theory. Andragogy (adult learning) is a theory that holds a set of assumptions about how adults learn. It uses approaches to learning that are problem based and cooperative rather than didactic (traditional lecturing or teacher "knows" model) and also recognizes more equality between the teacher and learner (Coquyt & Creasman, 2017, p. 100). It is very important that the relationship, right from the start, is perceived as colleague to colleague. This is easier said than done, and for some colleagues it might take a while to come around to this new relationship construct. Here are some tips when teaching about adult learning:

- Adults are autonomous and self-directed.
- Adults need to be free to direct their own learning.
- Adults bring knowledge and experience to each learning activity.
- Linking new material to learners' existing knowledge and experience creates a powerful and relevant learning experience.
- Adults need learning to be relevant and practical.
- Adults are problem oriented and want to apply what they've learned.

Above all else, adults want to be respected. A question to contemplate is the following:

1. How will you consider the elements of Adult Learning Theory in your new position?

Table 2.5.   Adult Learning Skills

Rate How Capable You Are with the Following Teacher Leader Skill (4) *Very Capable* (3) *Capable* (2) *Somewhat Capable* (1) *Not Capable at All*				
Adult Learning Theory	4	3	2	1

Based on what you know about your new position, how might you utilize this skill?

If this skill is considered a growth area (1 or 2), what can you do right now to improve your proficiency?

Listening/Collaboration

All leaders must be effective communicators, which requires that the leader is also a good listener. Teacher leaders are empowered to coach, mentor, and lead, all of which require that the teacher leader be accessible to others and available to listen, gather input, and provide meaningful feedback (Coquyt & Creasman, 2017, p. 103). Furthermore, listening invites diverse perspectives into the school's decision-making process. To sustain teacher leadership, conversations are critical, which require a certain level of respectful listening (Lambert, 2002).

Teacher leadership can help to create a culture of collaboration. Teacher leadership and collaboration are interconnected; in other words, they are inseparable, as both strengthen the other. Rosenholtz (as cited in Harris & Muijs, 2003) describes the unique relationship between collaboration and teacher leadership: "Collaboration is at the heart of teacher leadership, as it is premised upon change that is enacted collectively" (p. 40). We must not forget that teacher leadership is focused on improving student achievement by creating a culture that is based on collaboration. Questions to consider include:

1. How have you been given opportunities to develop listening skills through rich, real experiences? How might this serve you in your new position?
2. How often in the past were you given opportunities to lead through collaboration?

Table 2.6. Listening/Collaboration Skills

Rate How Capable You Are with the Following Teacher Leader Skill (4) *Very Capable* (3) *Capable* (2) *Somewhat Capable* (1) *Not Capable at All*			
Listening/Collaboration 4	3	2	1

Based on what you know about your new position, how might you utilize this skill?

If this skill is considered a growth area (1 or 2), what can you do right now to improve your proficiency?

Facilitation

Most teacher leaders will find themselves facilitating and/or leading some type of meeting as a function of their new leadership roles. A good facilitator is concerned with not only the outcome of the meeting or planning session but also how the people in the meeting participate and interact and also with the process (Coquyt & Creasman, 2017, p. 105). While achieving the goals and outcomes that everyone wants is of course important, a facilitator also wants to make sure that the process is sound, that everyone is engaged, and that the experience is the best it can be for the participants. A quality facilitator attends to every item listed each time he or she organizes a meeting:

1. makes sure everyone feels comfortable participating;
2. develops a structure that allows for everyone's ideas to be heard;
3. makes members feel good about their contribution to the meeting;
4. makes sure the group feels that the ideas and decisions are theirs, not just the leader/presenters;
5. supports everyone's ideas and does not criticize anyone for what they've said; and
6. remains neutral and never takes sides.

Some questions to ponder include:

1. Think about an instance in which the facilitator did, in your estimation, a fantastic job. What were some of the things he or she did to make the presentation so engaging?
2. Think about one that didn't go so smoothly. What were some of the things that could have been done better?

Table 2.7.   Facilitation Skills

Rate How Capable You Are with the Following Teacher Leader Skill (4) *Very Capable* (3) *Capable* (2) *Somewhat Capable* (1) *Not Capable at All*			
Facilitation	4	3	2	1

Based on what you know about your new position, how might you utilize this skill?

If this skill is considered a growth area (1 or 2), what can you do right now to improve your proficiency?

Reflection

Every teacher has no doubt heard at one time or another that he or she should be a reflective practitioner. I preach this in most every course that I teach at MSU Moorhead. In order to carry this conversation and analysis to a higher level, it is fitting to turn to John Dewey. In 1933, Dewey described the differences among impulsive action, routine action, and reflective action. The first, Dewey suggested, was based on trial and error. The second relied on more traditional ways of operating, oftentimes endorsed by authority.

However, Dewey claimed that reflective action arose from the work of educators who were active, who persistently and carefully considered how they practiced and what they were teaching, and was often the result of a need to solve a particular problem (Coquyt & Creasman, 2017, p. 107). According to Dewey (as cited in Coquyt & Creasman, 2017, p. 4), "Reflective thought is a chain [that] involves not simply a sequence of ideas but a consequence." Most teacher leaders are probably at either the impulsive or routine action stage described earlier. Ideally, the teacher leader would progress to the reflective action stage, but in order to do so the following questions should be considered:

Observation—How observant are you in regard to a) observing the behavior of others and b) observing how others respond to your behaviors?

Reasoning—How sensible or logical are you (or have you been in the past) in regard to educational topics, initiatives, and programs that directly affected you and your work here at the school?

- How do you respond to someone who is not thinking logically (too subjective) about a particular topic?

Responsibility—Your new role as a teacher leader has thrust many new responsibilities upon you. How do you think you will manage these new responsibilities?

- How comfortable have you been acting independently and making decisions without direct oversight?

Open Mindedness—How receptive are you (or have you been in the past) to the views and knowledge of others?

- How have you allowed others to express their views and recognized these views even though they might run contrary to your own?

Table 2.8. Reflection Skills

Rate How Capable You Are with the Following Teacher Leader Skill (4) *Very Capable* (3) *Capable* (2) *Somewhat Capable* (1) *Not Capable at All*			
Reflection 4	3	2	1

Based on what you know about your new position, how might you utilize this skill?

If this skill is considered a growth area (1 or 2), what can you do right now to improve your proficiency?

Modeling

Modeling describes the process of learning or acquiring new information, skills, or behavior through observation rather than through direct experience or trial and error efforts. Learning occurs as a function of observation rather than direct experience (Coquyt & Creasman, 2017, p. 108). Modeling is directly related to demonstrating or exhibiting the proper sequence or procedure. Many teacher leaders have and continue to use modeling in their classrooms when teaching certain topics. Showing students how to do something is a very powerful teaching strategy and is also a skill needed by teacher leaders in a variety of different areas.

Because it is impossible to define the venues that teacher leaders might use to practice modeling as a skill, let's turn to the Teacher Leader Model Standards to provide sample activities in which teacher leaders may find themselves modeling.

Domain 1/Function B: The teacher leader models effective skills in listening, presenting ideas, leading discussions, clarifying, mediating, and identifying the needs of self and others in order to advance shared goals and professional learning.

Domain 2: The teacher leader understands how research creates new knowledge, informs policies and practices, and improves teaching and learning. The teacher leader models and facilitates the use of systematic inquiry as a critical component of teachers' ongoing learning and development.

Domain 4: The teacher leader demonstrates a deep understanding of the teaching and learning processes and uses this knowledge to advance the professional skills of colleagues by being a continuous learner and modeling reflective practice based on student results. The teacher leader works collaboratively with colleagues to ensure instructional practices are aligned to a shared vision, mission, and goals.

Domain 6/Function B: The teacher leader models and teaches effective communication and collaboration skills with families and other stakeholders focused on attaining equitable achievement for students of all backgrounds and circumstances.

A question to ponder is the following:

1. In your current position, what are some things that might need to be modeled for your constituents?

Table 2.9. Modeling Skills

Rate How Capable You Are with the Following Teacher Leader Skill (4) *Very Capable* (3) *Capable* (2) *Somewhat Capable* (1) *Not Capable at All*				
Modeling	4	3	2	1

Based on what you know about your new position, how might you utilize this skill?

If this skill is considered a growth area (1 or 2), what can you do right now to improve your proficiency?

Big Picture

Teacher leadership at the surface is about empowering an individual to become a leader. However, as teacher leaders get comfortable with their new roles and continue to develop into school leaders, they garner a better understanding and recognition that it (teacher leadership) is about creating structures and a school culture that support the school's vision and student success (Coquyt & Creasman, 2017, p. 111). To be clear, teacher leadership must be intentionally invested in and associated with the school's vision. The vision for teacher leadership and school vision must work in unison to transform the school from one that is plagued by silos to one that is characterized by collaborative leadership structures.

Teacher leaders, like all quality leaders, realize that the positon is much larger than the individual who holds the position. They understand that their success is determined by their effectiveness in serving and empowering others and growing a culture that is conducive to shared, distributed, and collaborative leadership. Teacher leaders see the big picture past their positions and roles to exactly how they can help others and contribute in leading school transformation. To be successful, teacher leaders must remain focused on the work and the big picture of ensuring that students succeed. Questions to consider include:

1. Reflect on your school setting. How are teacher leaders encouraged to engage in professional growth that targets understanding the big picture?
2. How is big picture thinking and leading identified as a skill that needs further development in teacher leaders?
3. How do school administrators assist you in developing and growing leadership skills that will help you lead more effectively through big picture thinking?

Table 2.10.   Big Picture Skills

Rate How Capable You Are with the Following Teacher Leader Skill (4) *Very Capable* (3) *Capable* (2) *Somewhat Capable* (1) *Not Capable at All*			
Big Picture	4	3	2	1

Based on what you know about your new position, how might you utilize this skill?

If this skill is considered a growth area (1 or 2), what can you do right now to improve your proficiency?

Advocacy/Present Ideas

Cuthbertson (2014) states, "Seeing ourselves as teacher-leaders and advocates for public education is key. If we don't see ourselves in this role, we leave the door open for others outside the profession to tell our stories and determine the successes (and shortcomings) of our schools." Advocating can be as simple as having a one-on-one conversation with a parent or as detailed as preparing public comments and testifying before a local school board, state board of education, or other governing body.

Teacher leaders not only understand the processes needed to properly advocate for the needs of students but also understand how to obtain resources to support teaching and learning. The following five stages can be a helpful guide for teacher leaders to use when trying to secure additional resources.

1. Define objectives. What is it exactly that the group is advocating for?
2. Gather evidence to build an argument. What is it exactly that is needed?
3. Understand others' interests and resources. Are there other groups or individuals in the district with similar needs? Are there other groups or individuals that might have the resources you are seeking?
4. Present a clear case. Make certain the group you are presenting to understands exactly what you are advocating for and that the topic has been thoroughly investigated. If your group is presenting to the school board, be prepared to answer questions about cost, cross-curricular or multigrade applications, and demonstrate how what you are advocating for aligns with the district's vision and mission. If your group is presenting to a group of parents, understand that it is difficult for them to be objective. Focus on how it is going to support their child.
5. Amend your proposal based on the feedback obtained. Be prepared for this contingency. A teacher leader prepares for this possibility and has plan B already in the works (Coquyt & Creasman, 2017, pp. 113–14).

Questions to ponder include:

1. Which of the previous five steps are you familiar with and exercised in your previous efforts to advocate? Which are you unfamiliar with?
2. Do you see yourself performing this process in your current position? How so?
3. How will you go about discovering other groups with similar needs?

Table 2.11. Advocacy Skills

Rate How Capable You Are with the Following Teacher Leader Skill (4) *Very Capable* (3) *Capable* (2) *Somewhat Capable* (1) *Not Capable at All*			
Advocacy	4	3	2	1

Based on what you know about your new position, how might you utilize this skill?

If this skill is considered a growth area (1 or 2), what can you do right now to improve your proficiency?

Research

In my experience, the most common type of research that is performed in the PK–12 setting is action research. Ash and Persall (2000) define action research as the "implementation of innovative practices coupled with an assessment of those practices on student learning" (p. 15). Richard Sagor (2000) asserts,

> Practitioners who engage in action research inevitably find it to be an empowering experience. Action research has this positive effect for many reasons. Obviously, the most important is that action research is always relevant to the participants. Relevance is guaranteed because the focus of each research project is determined by the researchers, who are also the primary consumers of the findings. (p. 3)

Sagor has also outlined a seven-step process for performing action research in the educational setting:

1. *Select a focus.* Why does it merit further investigation?
2. *Clarify theories.* What values, beliefs, and theoretical perspectives do researchers hold relating to your focus? This is similar to performing a short literature review. Select at least three sources.

3. *Identify research questions*. Select one or two research questions.
4. *Collect data*. It is important here to use multiple sources of classroom data.
5. *Analyze data*. Answer the following questions: 1) What does the data say? 2) What is your interpretation of the data?
6. *Report results*. This can be done informally with your colleagues (at lunch, during a PLC) or formally (with administration).
7. *Take informed action*. Explain how your research will inform your teaching.

Questions to deliberate include:

1. How familiar are you with the action research process described here?
2. Has there been a need to perform action research recently at your school or grade level?

Table 2.12.   Action Research Skills

Rate How Capable You Are with the Following Teacher Leader Skill (4) *Very Capable* (3) *Capable* (2) *Somewhat Capable* (1) *Not Capable at All*				
Action Research	4	3	2	1

Based on what you know about your new position, how might you utilize this skill?

If this skill is considered a growth area (1 or 2), what can you do right now to improve your proficiency?

Although quite lengthy, the preceding section that focused on the particular skills teacher leaders must possess is, again, a good place to start for any novice teacher leader transitioning into a new role. The recommendation here is to begin developing a list of those skills that are essential and you can see yourself using on day one. Skills such as communication and organization often rise to the top. Next, list those skills that you believe will be important to hone and refine as you progress and learn more about your new role. Enough with the skills already. The final segment of this chapter will focus on what teacher leadership is all about.

KNOWLEDGE OF TEACHER LEADERSHIP

It came as no surprise that none of the teachers who participated in this study had a good working definition of teacher leadership. My experiences teaching and researching this topic have led me to believe that the words "teacher leader" have come to mean different things to different people and a strict definition of what constitutes a teacher leader is oftentimes difficult to find. In some schools teacher leaders are called "instructional coaches" and in others they are called "department chairs" or "subject leaders." The skills listed and examined in the previous section should provide some insight about exactly what it is that a teacher leader does in this position. Depending on the district or the position, certain skills may be needed or used more than others.

Another resource that was mentioned in the introduction was the Teacher Leader Model Standards. I have expanded on the list of domains (or standards) to include some of the functions contained in each domain that help explain and clarify the work of teacher leaders. A full list of domains and functions contained in the Teacher Leader Model Standards can be found in appendix D (on page 105).

The purpose of the next section is to provide the reader with examples of duties and responsibilities teacher leaders perform in their respective schools. It should be noted that the standards reflect fulfillment or the ultimate goal for teacher leaders. For example, changing Domain 1 to present tense might read, *Formation of a Collaborative Culture that Supports Teachers and Student Learning.*

Domain 1: Fostering a Collaborative Culture to Support Educator Development and Student Learning

• Collaboration with colleagues: listening skills, facilitation skills, presenting ideas, leading discussions
• Creation of an inclusive culture that welcomes diverse perspectives

Domain 2: Accessing and Using Research to Improve Practice and Student Learning

• Knowledge of "best practice" research about teaching effectiveness and student learning
• Analysis of student learning data

Domain 3: Promoting Professional Learning for Continuous Improvement

• Professional learning aligned to academic standards and school/district learning goals
• Knowledge of Adult Learning Theory
• Evaluation of effectiveness of current professional learning program

Domain 4:   Facilitating Improvements in Instruction and Student Learning

- Analysis of data to improve curriculum, instruction, assessment, school organization, and school culture
- Team leadership skills utilized to address curricular expectations and student learning needs
- Develop a reflective dialog with colleagues based on observations of instruction and student work

Domain 5:   Promoting the Use of Assessments and Data for School and District Improvement

- Increase the capacity of colleagues to identify and use multiple assessment tools aligned to academic standards
- Create a climate of trust and critical reflection to engage colleagues in challenging conversations about student learning data that leads to solutions to identified issues

Domain 6:   Improving Outreach and Collaboration with Families 'and Community

- Model and teach effective communication and collaboration skills with families and other stakeholders
- Use knowledge and understanding of the different backgrounds, ethnicities, cultures, and languages in the school community to promote effective interactions among colleagues, families, and the larger community

Domain 7:   Advocating for Student Learning and Profession

- Understand how educational policy is made at the local, state, and national level as well as the roles of school leaders, boards of education, legislators, and other stakeholders in formulating those policies
- Work with colleagues to identify and use research to advocate for teaching and learning processes that meet the needs of all students

Knowing what you do about your new teacher leader role, identify the domain and the function that is most closely related to what it is that you will be doing. Understand that the task description listed in the domains might not exactly match what it is that you will be doing. Some responsibilities and duties span more than one domain. Reflect upon the resources that you currently have and also the resources that you might need in order to perform the task adequately. Replicate table 2.13 as you see fit.

Table 2.13   Teacher Leader Domain/Function Self-Assessment

Domain and Function

Task Description

Resources Have/Need

Before leaving this section it is important to touch on something that I have found interesting during these past four years of teaching, reading, and researching teacher leadership. Each of the domains have been broken down in very simple terms or descriptions. I have asked my graduate students each semester, and also those who have participated in my previous research, to list each domain from most challenging to most benign. The results are not surprising. Domains 4 and 5 routinely rank as the most challenging to execute.

The question then is, why do so many administrators ask their new teacher leaders to focus on these demanding domains instead of the others? Wouldn't it make more sense to focus on one or two of the other domains initially and then slowly work toward domains 4 and 5? In some of my previous research there have been some instances of teacher leader burnout. It could be argued that a leading contributor to this burnout is the fact that the administration thrusts new teacher leaders into domains 4 and 5, and without proper training, the teacher leaders soon find themselves in over their heads. This is certainly a topic for another venue, but one that is worth exploring further.

CHAPTER SUMMARY

Two of the most important activities that can be performed during the "Moving In" phase are goal setting and keeping a journal. If this position is new to you and your school, goal setting is imperative! The goals that you and your administrator set prior to the beginning of the school year do not need to be extensive or detailed. This is because your goals will and should be revised and modified as you transition through the Moving Through phase and become not only more comfortable but also more knowledgeable about what it is that you really should be doing. Here are some sample goals from one of the teacher leaders who participated in this study.

Goal 1:   Create a short but detailed description of my new position.
Goal 2:   Develop a schedule for when I will meet with and visit the
              classrooms of the teachers I will be working with.
Goal 3:   Develop a form for teachers to use that identify strengths/
              weaknesses, needs, and personal goals.
Goal 4:   Develop a list of topics for monthly meetings with administration.
Goal 5:   Begin collecting books or periodicals about teacher leadership.

The importance of goal setting and revising your goals as you become more familiar with what it is that you need to do is imperative and something that will be reexamined in chapter 4 during the latter half of the Moving Through phase. An interesting feature missing from most of the goals teacher leaders set for themselves in this early stage is location.

Set goals for yourself that put you where the action is, in classrooms, hallways, lunchrooms, and teachers' lounges. It is imperative that your routine stay as similar to the classroom teachers' schedules as possible. Your ultimate goal is for your colleagues to see you as one of them but performing a job that is a little different. A final goal that needs to be on every list is this: *Demonstrate to those I am working with that I am still one of them and not part of the administrative team.* This will prove to be easier said than done but not impossible to achieve.

One of the teachers who participated in this study decided to keep a weekly journal that described what she did each day and summarized what she accomplished at the end of each week. In the introduction it was recommended that the "Self-Reflection" segments in each chapter should, at the very least, find their way into your personal journal. It is highly recommended that each new teacher leader keep a journal throughout the entire year. Related to this, portion out fifteen to twenty minutes a day to reflect and write down events and activities you performed during the day. Some of these activities will be planned and some will be related to your goals, but it will be surprising how many activities you find yourself doing that materialize out of thin air.

Chapter 3

Moving Through

Ignorance Is Bliss

In the introduction the reader might recall that the outline for each chapter, including the timeline for each interview, was established. See appendix A (on page 93) for a refresher. Chapter 3 examines the time period from the second week of the new school year up to the last week of October. It was at this time that the first of two interviews were performed during the "Moving Through" phase. Of utmost interest was to uncover how the first few months of school had gone for our new teacher leaders. One thing that should be established is that there was not a scientific formula or theory that was followed in the decision to use the first few months (around eight weeks) as the end of one phase and the beginning of another.

This decision was made by falling back on twenty-three years of experience working in PK–12 education. In my experience as a classroom teacher and administrator, the first couple of weeks of the new school year are a dream for most. As a teacher it is a time when everything in the building and classroom is fresh and clean and all of your students are relatively happy and, maybe most importantly, all of them are passing their classes. As an administrator, there are no "fires" to be put out at the beginning of the school year and you can fall back on more mundane managerial tasks rather than those that require either long-term planning or quick decisions.

For the new teacher leaders, their new world is somewhere in between teacher and new administrator. Gone is what had become routine, customary, and safe (that being their role as classroom teachers). What they now face is a future that is uncertain, and there are probably more questions than answers. It is not uncommon for new teacher leaders to feel a bit lost or abandoned during the early weeks of the school year. TLA put it this way: "I felt like I was waiting for something to happen. The activities I planned to do needed other teachers or my principal to be involved and they were pretty busy." Teachers are busy doing "their thing" in the classrooms, getting to know their students, assimilating them into the classroom environment, establishing procedures and routines, introducing new topics, and giving detailed explanations about important topics that are included in the current subject.

Administrators are even busier now than the teachers. I recall quite vividly how blissful the summer months were for an administrator. Summer was a time to plan and prepare. A former boss of mine, Scott Monson, used to say, "Plan the work, then work the plan." Working the plan proved to be a little more challenging. Even the best laid plans get pushed to the side once the teachers and students arrive in school.

During this time (first two weeks of school) the administrator is busy appeasing everyone. At least that was my experience. Those plans that were worked on, improved upon, and finalized during the summer have been pushed aside in favor of more pressing issues like tweaking student schedules, setting up meetings, and answering myriad questions from parents. Add to this mix a new teacher leader or two and things get a little more complex.

Any administrator who is worth his or her salt would have in place a first-month plan for the new teacher leader. Every administrator is different, so what they have planned for teacher leaders in district A may be quite different from their colleague in district B. If there is no plan, my advice to the new teacher leader is to do the plan yourself. This idea of empowerment was presented in the introductory section in chapter 2.

Build a daily activity chart where you detail everything you will be doing for the first week of school. Make sure that every hour or half-hour is accounted for. Provide a detailed description of what you will be doing, where you will be, who you will be meeting with, and the purpose of what you are doing. As was stated in chapter 1, teacher leaders have initiative. A sample morning schedule is shown in appendix C on page 103.

Creating the plan is step one. Step two is scheduling a meeting with your administrator. This meeting needs to occur on the first day of school. Share your plan with your administrator and provide great detail for the activities, demonstrate how they align with your new position, and make certain to have any meetings scheduled with other staff arranged and ready to go. You really have nothing to lose. Any meeting you have previously arranged can be bumped for the boss, so to speak, and rescheduled for a later date.

At the end of this chapter you should become more familiar with and will be better prepared to resolve the following:

• Develop a basic understanding of psychosocial competence and how this is related to self-esteem and personal worth.

- Working with adults is very different from working with students. It is important to gain a practical definition of Adult Learning Theory.
- The comfort zone that you settled into as a classroom teacher will probably remain elusive in your first few months on the job in your new role.

PULSE CHECK

Before we get too deep in the weeds it is important to revisit the Four Ss summary table and explain which factors were analyzed during each phase and also which were not investigated at all. We will begin with the latter. As was stated in the introduction, it behooves anyone who is transitioning into a different position or role to examine and reflect upon all Four Ss and their corresponding factors.

It stands to reason that not all factors will be related to each S, depending on the stage of transition. A perfect example of this is the factor (gain or loss) associated with one of the Four Ss, Situation. In the "Moving In" phase, this question (Do you see this transition as a gain or a loss?) is very hard if not impossible to determine. A richer analysis could be made at some time, probably toward the later stages of the "Moving Through" phase. This reasoning (Does it fit or is it appropriate?) is used throughout the examination of each phase. Once again, there is no scientific formula or theory to substantiate this reasoning, only twenty-three years of experience and three to four years researching, teaching, and writing about teacher leadership.

Some of the *factors* were not investigated at all during the "Moving In" phase. These include:

Self-Control, Options, Stage of Life,
Strategies, Changed View of Situation/Flexibility

The decision not to examine these factors had more to do with the type of research that was being conducted than the value of investigating each factor. Qualitative research relies heavily on analyzing the "lived" experience of the subjects using an emergent design. For example, in the early stages, the new teacher leader has very little <u>Control</u> over what is required of him or her nor what exactly it is that he or she should be doing. This control increases through experience and time. During the "Moving Through" phase, teacher leaders have more control over what they do on a daily basis and are in a position to offer suggestions to the administration regarding how to better spend their time and what they should be focusing on.

Regarding <u>Stage of Life</u>, all of the participants in the study had ten years or more of classroom teaching experience. It is safe to state that all of the participants were approached by their building administrators to consider making this transition. One participant was looking for something different at this stage of her life. The rest were content with their classroom teaching positions.

Similarly, Options could be investigated early on; each teacher leader had the option of accepting this new role or staying in the classroom and obviously they all decided to transition into their new positions. In the Moving Out phase, each was afforded the option of continuing on in their current position or returning to the classroom. Additional research as to why they decided to remain in their teacher leadership position or leave will be left to and merit future research. Appendix A provides a visual for which factors were investigated during each phase. Table 3.1 lists those factors that were scrutinized during the first interview in the "Moving In" phase.

Table 3.1.   Interview #2

Factors	Moving Through (MT) *Second Week to the End of October*
Situation	None
Self	
Strengths/Weaknesses	X
Previous Experience/Adaptability	X
Support	
Spouse/Partner/Family	X
Workspace—Physical Setting	X
Co-Workers	X
Institutional and Other Organizations	X
Strategies—Coping	
Psycho—Self-Esteem/Personal Worth	X
Cope Well in Different Settings	X
Goal Setting	X
Planning	X
Health	X
Balance/Flexibility	X

Self-Reflection

• Have you utilized the Four Ss (or similar) material in the past during the contemplation period prior to making some type of professional transition? If so, how did this prepare you for your new venture? If you answered no, how might you use this and Schlossberg's theory in your future position?
• How have the goals you set during the summer months portion of the "Moving In" stage changed as you have begun settling into your new position?

RESEARCH QUESTIONS AND
EXPLANATIONS OF FINDINGS

As table 3.1 illustrates, the second interview covers quite a bit of ground. Of utmost importance during this early "Moving Through" phase was an in-depth study of the factors *Situation, Support,* and *Strategies.* To reiterate, this second interview took place during the end of October. This allowed the new teacher leaders a little bit of time to ease into and reflect on their new positions.

Psychosocial

Schlossberg (1981) asserts that psychosocial competence is divided into three areas: self-attitude, world attitude, and behavioral attitude (p. 12). Under the umbrella of self-attitude is also a focus on self-esteem and personal worth. World attitude will be examined in later chapters by analyzing optimism and trust. In addition, Schlossberg argued that the other factors affect adaptation, including "an active coping orientation; high initiative; realistic goal setting; substantial planning, forbearance and effort in the service of attaining goals; and a capacity for enjoying success" (p. 12). The behavioral attitude is defined as an active coping orientation, high initiative, and realistic goal setting.

Common themes that were discerned after analyzing the interview data were the importance of past success, a search for affirmation and trust, and the importance of setting goals. Other themes discovered included the importance of spousal support, the establishment of regular professional group meetings, and some early challenges working with adults.

All of the teacher leaders responded positively to the question about psychosocial competence. It was interesting that in their responses they discussed their successes as classroom teachers first. Some used words or phrases like "kindness," "strong work ethic," and "self-esteem" in their answers. Regarding self-esteem, TLC commented,

> This job has been tough on my self-esteem at times. Staff members can say snide remarks about the fact that I am not in the classroom anymore and what is it that I do all day. This can be hard to take some days.

Most clearly believed that they were still learning the nuances of their new positions. Empathy came up more than once. TLA responded,

> I consider myself to be a highly empathetic individual, which I believe has been a strong contributor to my success in the classroom. The downside of being highly empathetic is that the extra sensitivity may cause me to be highly

sensitive to non-verbals, which means I can read into situations which may or may not be true.

TLB asserted,

I wish I had more confidence and tools in my belt to be able to handle a teacher who is not asking for help but clearly needs it. I am working on this skill, but definitely am not real comfortable in this area yet.

TLD summarized his thoughts about self-esteem by stating the following:

I have a strong sense of personal worth. I am in this occupation because I truly believe that I am making a difference, even if it is in one student, and now one teacher's life. The projects, conversations, and curriculum into which I am pouring my time, energy, and talents are gauged according to the usefulness in someone's life.

Cope Well with Different Settings/Goal Setting

As was mentioned previously, most teachers made comments about how they liked challenges and described this new position as yet another challenge. Most teachers seemed to be doing fine coping with their new positions. TLD asserted,

This year, more than any other, has proven to me that this statement (I cope well in different situations) is true for me. I have been out of my comfort zone so many times that I have lost count, but I feel as though I have been landing on my feet. Basic human relations skills (kindness, respect, listening) are universal in any situation, including this one.

In regard to goal setting, most of the teachers had established goals they wanted to achieve by the end of the term. Most understandably needed to go back and reevaluate the goals they set for themselves early on during the summer. TLA commented, "Sometimes I meet them, other times it is good just to look back at what I thought I wanted to accomplish, but needed to reevaluate the direction I was heading." She also offered,

So far, I have set three goals for this term. Thus far, I have been able to make progress on these goals. I have kept the list visible so I have to see it every day. I figure that if I want teachers to set goals, I need to do it myself.

TLE admitted to putting too much on her plate: "I have a hard time saying no and have worked on setting boundaries and managing my workload."

Planning/State of Health

All of the teachers reported that they considered themselves very accomplished at planning. Most mentioned time management, attention to detail, task completion, and organization in their answers. TLE offered, "Planning in this new position takes on a whole new meaning." A classroom teacher who has taught the same subject for a period of five years can easily plan for what he or she will be doing as well as what his or her students will be doing at any time during the year. The veteran teacher has time and experience on his or her side. For most any unit he or she will be teaching, he or she has answered almost all of the questions he or she will be asked and has a good understanding of topics the students will easily comprehend and those he or she will need to spend a bit more time on.

TLC commented, "Sometimes it is hard to plan for something you know nothing about." TLD offered, "My plans are often interrupted by things I had no idea were heading my way." For the most part "things" were oftentimes associated with the amount of time they spent on certain items like learning new curriculum, the curriculum process, the teacher's contract, and how to be tactful and diplomatic when talking with their colleagues.

All but one commented that they were in a good state of health. This teacher explained that the added stress of her son getting married over the holiday break contributed to her response about health. "I am in the worst shape I have been in a long time. I am not exercising regularly, and I know this is a problem." She vowed to begin exercising again after the wedding when she could devote more time to it.

Spouse/Workspace or Physical Setting

All of the teachers responded that their greatest support system was their spouses. TLA commented, "My husband has always been my best cheerleader. He thinks I can do anything, no matter the challenge, and he believes I will conquer it." TLB stated, "My husband has been great. He reminds me about the other side of things, things that are not in my direct view, yet is very supportive of me as well." TLE commented that she has a very strong family and friend base. She asserted, "I have leaned on them for support as I navigate this new job, new stresses, and new challenges."

Schlossberg (1981) asserted that physical setting is a broad category. Physical setting can include "climate, weather, urban or rural location, neighborhood, living arrangements, and workplace" (p. 11). The focus for this study will be the physical setting in the school they work at. TLA commented, "I love where my new office is. I am in the mix with the other teachers and I am very close to our newest teacher for him to pop in for quick advice or larger concerns."

TLB stated, "I have a great workspace. I am still with my peeps and the room is private and has everything I need to accomplish the tasks I need to." One teacher was not as enthused about her office area. She stated, "I share an office with four other people and I literally share a desk. I miss having my own space."

Co-Workers/Institutional

One aspect that is unique in this study is that two of the participants were hired at the same time and went through this transition together. Both reported that they lean on each other greatly in good times and in bad. TLB commented,

> Having another teacher leader has been awesome. She and I are learning this as we go and when I am down or frustrated she is the first one I go to. When I have a great day, she is the first one I tell.

The other teacher, TLA, stated, "I am so thankful. If I didn't have her, I would be very alone. I would have no one to brainstorm with or vent to." She went on to state, "If you have one teacher leader in your building, you need two." The others responded that it is difficult going through the transition alone. TLE commented, "Who can support me in this situation? Most people don't get this job." A saving grace for some of the teachers was the institution of a monthly meeting where all of the new teacher leaders and instructional coaches in the district came together to collaborate and learn. TLA commented, "I love attending our monthly meetings. I learn a lot from others who have been doing this job a lot longer than I have."

Another teacher leader looked at these meetings as an opportunity to share in a safe place. He asserted, "We can discuss things that come up in our classrooms or in our schools, good or bad. It is nice to have a venue to share frustrations." This same teacher leader stressed the importance of having elementary, middle, and secondary teacher leaders together in the same room. "It is important to have conversations with those in a similar situation, but different, if you know what I mean. There are a lot of differences between what happens in the elementary compared to the high school."

Strengths/Weakness and Challenges

In this interview it was important to go beyond some of the perceived strengths (planning, goal setting) to determine the teachers' perception of how they had grown as leaders during this time. A couple of the teachers offered that this question might be better asked of those with whom they had been working. TLA asserted, "I am more focused on the quality of integrity than ever before. Ethos has always been important to me in working with kids, and it's no different now in working with adults." This particular teacher chose to focus specifically on confidentiality and choice by stating,

> First, I remain committed to confidentiality. I will not share what a teacher and I discuss or work on with another teacher or [administrator]. It's our project, and it stays between us. Secondly, I am still committed to the concept of teacher choice. To explain, I am less likely to directly tell a teacher what they need to do. I offer suggestions, but ultimately it is their classroom and they need to decide if they will take my advice. I feel as though this is the best way for me to maintain a good, professional, respectful working relationship.

One teacher leader spoke to the fact that she felt she was becoming more assertive with her interactions with other teachers and shared with me a Personal Evaluation Form she had begun using. Another teacher leader shared with me samples of her weekly email communication to all of her teachers as well as a feedback loop of reflections and questions that drive her "next steps." This particular teacher looked at this as an important first step toward creating a culture in her school in which teacher voice is valued more than ever. She offered, "It is very important that the group of teachers I am working with feel like they have a contact person to ask questions of, one who will provide feedback, and seek clarification."

Finally, one teacher commented about something that she struggled with early on but has become much better at: having difficult conversations. She shared,

> I was able to successfully address some changes that needed to occur in the classroom through careful questioning. I begin the conversations with sentence stems like can you . . . I wonder . . . how do you decide . . . I'm curious to know . . . what will be the effect if? I have been successful in getting teachers to think, reflect, and draw conclusions on their own.

Each teacher shared that he or she is faced with many different challenges in his or her new roles. TLA stated, "Every time I feel like I have a sense of where I am going, something comes along and interferes with what I had planned." The nuances of working with adults were brought up on a couple of different occasions. One teacher stated, "My greatest challenge has been walking the fine line in working with adults." TLE asserted,

> The behavior of certain adults has been the most challenging, devastating, and eye opening. I have been floored at some of the disrespect, entitlements, and rudeness that have come with some of my work. I have been continually heart-broken

by the amount of educators I have seen who are looking for short-cuts or solutions that meet their own needs and not necessarily the needs of their students.

Balance

The question about balance during this phase is different from Schlossberg's assumption (balance of resources to deficits) mentioned earlier in this book. Finding balance is very important in any job, and as TLC stated, "I feel like my schedule is constantly changing, unpredictable, and hard to plan for. I haven't found a balance." For most teachers, finding time and balancing their time was a constant chore. The silver lining was that at least for some, finding a balance in their new role is becoming a reality. TLB noted,

> Little by little I am learning to divide up my time. I am still working on polishing up on the procedural things. I still want my main job to be working with teachers and helping them become more efficient with their students. However, since developing relationships and trust has taken longer than I thought, I've needed to evolve.

Another teacher shared,

> I think I am doing well with balance. Early on, I came across a sample calendar that purposely showed coaches what they need to literally pencil into their schedules. The three things are research, reading, and reflection. I have this calendar on my wall and literally pencil in research, reading, and reflecting on my schedule. Currently, I have scheduled 50–75% of my time to work with teachers.

KEY TAKEAWAYS AND RECOMMENDATIONS

As stated previously, there were many elements to this early "Moving In" phase that were analyzed and an equal number of themes that emerged from the data. Rather than bogging the reader down with a dissection of each, the focus will be limited to just a few. The four elements that merit further scrutiny are *Comfort Zone, Scheduled Meetings, Working with Adults,* and *Balancing Resources to Deficits.*

Comfort Zone

How long does it take for someone to experience his or her comfort zone? As an administrator working with new teachers during their induction period before fall workshop, this topic was discussed at length. I took this opportunity to share my opinion that it takes at least three years to find your comfort zone as a teacher. After three years you can starting thinking about moving up in the coaching ranks, increasing your involvement with various committees, and seeking out leadership positions within the school district.

During the interviews with the new teacher leaders, when the term "comfort zone" came up, almost all of them reminisced about their successes as classroom teachers. In this environment they were comfortable, confident, and knowledgeable about the subjects they were teaching. Transitioning into a totally different position brought all of them back to ground zero. None of them had any idea what it felt like to be in that comfort zone as a teacher leader.

Good advice to new teacher leaders is to remain patient. Although my role in this situation was that of the researcher and not administrator, the advice was offered anyway. The conversation then shifted to doing your best work in any position. Oftentimes your best work will happen only when you become comfortable with your current position. This will take time. As the reader might recall from the introduction, one of the four characteristics of teacher leaders is *invested*. Invested teachers are in it for the long haul.

Colleagues

In chapter 2 the reader was provided with some insight into the differences between working with adults and working with students as well as a brief examination of Adult Learning Theory. It was also cited in the introduction that one of the characteristics of teacher leaders is a good understanding of Adult Learning Theory. Two concerns were uncovered in the research. One was power and the other was confidentiality. Most of the new teacher leaders struggled with both early in their tenure.

Power, taken in the proper context, is specifically evaluative power. For some reason the classroom teachers believed that the teacher leaders had evaluative powers similar to those of the administration. Confidentiality also came up numerous times when the teacher leaders discussed their relationships with their colleagues. During classroom visits, if something in the classroom appeared to be off or the teacher leader observed something egregious with either teaching or pedagogy, the teacher leaders admitted that it was difficult for them not to make the administration aware.

Once again, patience is the mantra. The topic of the administrative role will be dealt with later in this book. One of the many roles or duties of the administration right from the start is to make clear that teacher leaders are *not* administrators; teacher leaders are quite the opposite actually. The administration must make clear to all staff that if teacher leaders are in their classroom, they are not there to evaluate their teaching performance.

If a teacher leader is put into a position in which he or she witnesses something deficient or incomplete regarding the teaching or pedagogy, it is best that he or she schedules a meeting or talk informally with that teacher about it. Only after time has passed and the classroom teacher has not been disparaged by the administrator will the colleagues realize that what is discussed between them and the teacher leader is in the strictest confidence. This is a marathon, not a sprint.

One recommendation, and probably a good exercise at this stage of the game, is to revisit appendix B (on page 95). If you recall, this table summarizes the *Nine Characteristics of High-Performing Schools*. What is important here are the words that describe the actions or activities of an educational leader (administrator) compared to those of teacher leaders. Develop a short list of actions that are administrative in nature, such as

- monitors and evaluates
- builds and sustains
- collects and analyzes
- develops and implements

To a lesser extent, you might be assisting the administration in some of these activities, but most of your time should be spent performing the following with the classroom teachers:

- assisting
- facilitating
- supporting
- collaborating
- advocating

Scheduled Meetings

Aside from being *invested* and having a good working knowledge of Adult Learning Theory, teacher leaders have *initiative*. Before moving forward it should also be pointed out that previously, in chapter 2, the *innovative* idea to develop a detailed schedule to follow for the first two weeks of school was suggested (appendix C). The same principle applies here. Coquyt and Creasman (2017) advise administrators to schedule individual meetings with each teacher leader at least once per month. Another suggestion was to have all teacher leaders in the district meet at least once per month as well.

If meetings (individual or group) are not planned by the administration, there is no reason why the teacher leaders employed at the school or district cannot schedule their own meetings. It has been said that the best form of staff development is to have teachers talking to other teachers about teaching. If you are the only teacher leader in your district, check the surrounding districts and see if there is interest from any of their teacher leaders to meet on a regular basis.

Balance Resources with Deficits

As stated in the introduction, an *assertive* teacher leader has a good working knowledge of the bureaucracy of the school and district in which he or she works. This knowledge can be used to acquire certain resources that will be needed to effectively do the job of the new position. Unfortunately, if the teacher leader does not have a good handle on the scope of his or her responsibilities and duties, it is next to impossible to know exactly which resources you have and which you may want to acquire.

The second greatest resource you will have as a teacher leader is other teacher leaders. Together you can share or brainstorm such things as schedules, plans for working with teachers in their department, and research articles or quality textbooks about teacher leadership. The greatest resource you have at your disposal is *you*. Most of the teacher leaders that were interviewed had previously been classroom teachers for over ten years. Simply start by thinking about what it was that you believed you needed in order to do a better job teaching. Develop a short list and start with that. If anything else, this short list will be a good ice breaker for when you start meeting with the teachers you will be working with.

CHAPTER SUMMARY

The early part of the "Moving Through" phase can be overwhelming for the new teacher leader, to say the least. One common theme running throughout this phase is that it seemed like most of the teacher leaders were spending a lot of time doing things (fill in the blank here) for other people. Granted, if you are performing duties and responsibilities developed by you and your administrator, those are on you. A word of caution: Pay close attention to what it is that you say you will do for the classroom teachers you engage with on a daily basis. Chances are that you are busy enough trying to manage getting pulled in a variety of different directions coupled with learning the nuances of your new position.

This situation, shouldering some of the responsibilities and finding answers to some concerns your colleagues might have, should be avoided at all costs. How many times has this already happened to you? It is quite easy to do, actually. In my previous life as a PK–12 administrator, this happened to me a lot, especially during my first year. The act of walking down the hallway would elicit at least five questions, comments, or concerns from various faculty members. The fastest way for me to get to my destination was to tell them to come see me later on, or worse yet, that I would look into it and get back to them later.

What would happen in many of these situations is that I would spend my precious time finding answers to their questions, consider the comments and put them on the back burner, and then attempt to find possible solutions to their concerns. This all took time, valuable time that could be spent on more pressing matters. After a while, a system was developed in which if I was "cornered" in the hallway, I would respectfully recommend that the teacher schedule an appointment with my secretary and we could discuss his or her issue at a later date and time. This system actually accomplished two things.

The first was that the ball was put back in his or her court, so to speak. If his or her concern was truly important, he or she would schedule a meeting. If it wasn't, no meeting was scheduled but I would informally discuss this with him or her at a later date. The second was it gave me time to carefully consider the request. Was the issue really his or her responsibility or obligation? Was the problem a fundamental component of his or her teaching duties? I made certain that I would assist, guide, and direct him or her to the proper resources to the best of my ability, but I would not assume something that is his or her responsibility.

A tremendous resource for anyone interested in developing strategies to ensure that everyone is doing their fair share is Todd Whitaker's (2012) book *Shifting the Monkey*. Whitaker asserts, "Monkeys are the responsibilities, obligations, and problems everyone deals with every day. You can easily handle your share of normal monkeys, but you can just as easily become overwhelmed when you get stuck shouldering other people's inappropriate monkeys" (p. 3).

Chapter 4

Moving Through

The Search for Affirmation

Chapter 4 might seem a little light compared to the earlier chapters. Quite possibly this was due to the fact that as a qualitative researcher one starts to feel a little too intrusive and that the subjects should be left alone for a while. The second interview was quite intense and it occurred what seemed like only a short time ago. This third interview was intentionally designed to be short, quick, and to serve as a check in, so to speak.

Earlier in this book it was explained that the Four Ss table and the accompanied factors align or do not align with the dates or timeframe of a typical school year. Quite simply, certain factors could not be measured because the new teacher leaders had not experienced them yet. Gain or loss was the example used previously in the "Moving In" phase. It is hard to determine if the transition into a new role is seen as a gain or a loss in the first few months on the job.

By the time the third interview was scheduled in late January, early February, almost all of the factors could be assessed. In the interest of time, all of the factors could have been evaluated at this point, but I decided against it. By the fifth month in their new positions, most teacher leaders had experienced challenges and successes and thankfully all had fallen into a somewhat manageable routine. Almost all of the teacher leaders had established and revised their personal goals on a monthly basis and shared with the administration how they had accomplished some of these goals through trial and tribulation. Some of the earlier concerns expressed by the classroom teachers had now been settled for the most part. At this juncture I was very interested to examine factors associated with Situation that could not be investigated before. For example:

- How optimistic are you on most days?
- Do you see this new position as a gain or a loss?

- Was this a positive or negative move?
- How long can you see yourself doing this?

Table 4.1.   Interview #3

Factors	Moving Through (MT) Late January/Early February
Situation	
New Role	X
Positive or Negative?	X
Gain or Loss?	X
Duration	X
Self	
Strengths/Weaknesses	X
Control	X
Resiliency	X
Options	X
Stage of Life	X
Support	None
Strategies—Coping	
Optimistic—Hope	X
Manage Emotions and Stress	X

PULSE CHECK

How do you know if you are doing a good job in your current position? In the university system I currently work in, all professors are required to develop a Professional Development Plan (PDP). This plan clarifies how each professor is going to fulfill the requirements associated with a variety of different criteria. Some of the criteria include effectiveness in teaching, scholarly works, and evidence of continued preparation and study.

At the end of the year a Professional Development Report (PDR) is developed. The PDR explains in great detail what was done throughout the year to meet the criteria listed on the PDP. The PDR also contains evidence that substantiates that certain goals within each criteria were met. A committee of your peers and the college dean approve both the PDP and the PDR. Positive remarks on the PDR signify proficiency.

Classroom teachers are able to determine if they are successful in their current positions in a variety of different ways. For some, having students visit with them after school about the subject(s) being taught affirms that the students not only understand the material but also want to know more. Seeing an improvement in student behaviors, rising scores on daily homework assignments, and increased test scores are also signs of quality teaching. Performing well in front of the administrator and receiving favorable scores and feedback after a formal classroom observation is also a pretty good sign that one is doing a good job.

One of the recurring themes throughout this latter "Moving Through" stage was a need for affirmation. The teacher leaders didn't come right out and say it, but they wanted to know from administration if they were doing a good job. They wanted to know if there were certain facets of the job they should be working harder at or should be paying more attention to. A few of the teacher leaders were becoming a little frustrated because they were not seeing the types of results they thought they should with some of the teachers they were working with.

They were probably being a little too hard on themselves. A simple question asked of one of the teacher leaders at some juncture of the interview helped in my understanding of how he or she was feeling at this particular time. The question was, "how do you know?"

It became very apparent that personal goal setting is only one facet in the search for affirmation. Quite honestly, it is only one of two factors in any search for affirmation. The other part is some form of measurement criteria that can be used to measure effectiveness or achievement. One can only get a true picture of affirmation or verification that one is doing a quality job when both facets are considered at the same time. As a qualitative researcher, my focus is constantly on the "why" rather than the "what" of social phenomena. Coupled with this is the reliance on the direct experiences of human beings as meaning-making agents in their everyday lives.

The "why" in this particular situation is how the teacher leaders perceived their new situation based on their feelings and personal goals. The "what" in this situation is some form of measurements or standards that serve as some type of quantitative device. It became apparent that it would be very difficult to get an accurate understanding of the "essence" of this stage without considering both.

In the examples mentioned earlier, classroom teachers and university professors can rely on their personal perceptions of how well they believe they are performing in their current roles. What affirms and supports these perceptions is some type of measurement instrument. The primary method used to evaluate the effectiveness of classroom teachers is the formal observation approach. Essentially, the administrator spends a predetermined period of time in the teacher's classroom and analyzes his or her teaching using some type of measurement tool.

As was previously stated, university professors, in my experience, use the PDP/PDR process. My "aha" moment occurred with the realization that there was no formal way, other than personal goals, to measure the effectiveness of what these teachers were doing for the past five months. In the "Key Takeaways" section of this chapter a sample evaluation plan, similar to the PDP/PDR process explained earlier, is outlined. This plan, which could and *should be used* as a way to evaluate the effectiveness of teacher leaders, uses the Teacher Leader Model Standards as a framework for the fundamental outline and design.

Self-Reflection

- How long into your first year of teaching did it take for you to realize that this is the type of job that you can see yourself doing for a long time?
- Were there times, in previous jobs, when you thought you couldn't endure but continued to soldier on? What was it that you did that pushed you past the difficult times?
- Are there more factors from Support that are more necessary during the "Moving Through" phase than the "Moving In" phase?

RESEARCH QUESTIONS AND
EXPLANATION OF FINDINGS

By the time the third interview occurred, the teacher leaders had been in their new roles for around five months. The primary focus of the interview was on Self and I specifically wanted to investigate the questions they still had about their role, how much control they felt they had, options available to do other things, resiliency, and their general perception of their new roles.

Questions

This portion of the interview focused on questions that the teachers have now that they didn't think about when they began in their new roles. In an indirect way, the questions they came up with could be labeled concerns or challenges. I thought it was important for the teacher leaders to come up with some of the questions and put them in the driver's seat, so to speak. I allowed them to speak freely and did not push them to come up with solutions or to find the answers. Although they were not prompted, almost every question they had was directed toward the administration. The questions were either personal (I or me) or involved guidance (how would you/how do you) questions.

Personal

1. How am I doing?
2. Am I anywhere close to the expectations that you had regarding my role in this position?
3. When is it time for me to take my concerns to the administration about a teacher I am working with?

Guidance

1. How do you hold teachers accountable for being empathetic and kind to students and parents?
2. How do you challenge teachers to adjust and change who have continually shown practices that are not developmentally appropriate for their students?
3. What are your greatest frustrations as an administrator?

The first two personal questions speak directly to one of the major themes mentioned earlier, the search for affirmation. The third question introduces a circumstance that is vital to the success of developing and using teacher leaders in any school district. Classroom teachers who are not performing effectively in their current positions are undeniably an administrative concern and not something that should be managed by the teacher leader.

All good administrators schedule time to be in the classrooms either formally or informally and are constantly assessing what is being taught, how it is being taught, and how well the students are learning. The teacher leader needs to trust that his or her administrator is aware of the situation and that the deficiencies are being addressed. Moreover, the trusting relationships that have been established between teacher leader and classroom teacher need to continue at all costs.

This classroom performance topic is also observed in the first and second (guidance) questions about accountability and how the administrator manages those teachers who are not willing to change their classroom and instructional practices. Once again, it is not the job of the teacher leader to handle these administrative and evaluative tasks.

Optimistic

All of the teachers reported that they considered themselves to be very optimistic. At this stage in their new roles, it was clear that some were searching for affirmation; most were working through trust issues, while others were developing strategies to cope with the minutiae of their new roles. Through it all, all still seemed relatively optimistic by the time the third interview was scheduled.

TLE remarked, "There are days I am not sure I am doing any good. I long for the days when I accomplished tasks like knowing I helped a student learn something new." TLA commented, "I have learned that even though you thought you were speaking in confidence that is not always the case. I have learned I need to have guarded trust with some of my co-workers." Regarding trust, TLB remarked, "I trust that the teachers with whom I work know the answers to their own problems. My job is to support them as they find solutions." Finally, TLA made the following remark that indicated her strategy when it comes to problem solving:

> I almost always play the role of devil's advocate to make sure that all sides of a situation are considered. In this position, I find myself playing angel's advocate. When a colleague feels discouraged or hits a roadblock, I have taken to finding at least one positive aspect. In this position, I support teachers, and often that support comes in the form of simple encouragement.

Stress

Central to this study is the degree of stress that accompanied this transition into a new role. All of the teachers indicated that there was some degree of stress, some more than others. The common denominator seemed to be a lack of expectations and being pushed out of their comfort zone. TLD commented, "My new role has caused me stress. I would say it is slightly higher than when I was a teacher." TLA stated similarly, "The new role has caused me lots of stress but also a new awareness of the complexities of a public education system." TLB summarized her anxiety by stating,

> My stress level has increased because I often feel pushed out of my comfort zone. I get pulled into situations about which I have limited or no knowledge [working with the Special Education department or the English Language Learners teachers]. However, I am learning and learning quickly. The key has been to be humble and say, I don't know and be a good listener and note taker. I feel unsettled because I just don't know what to expect out of the teachers I am working with and also with the leadership.

Gain or Loss

Some but not all transitions require a role change (Schlossberg, 1981). Schlossberg posits, "Regardless of whether a transition involves a role gain or loss, some degree of stress accompanies it" (p. 8). There was not a consensus in the answers to the question about whether the transition into a new position was seen as a gain or a loss. Interestingly, only two of the participants indicated that at this point they could see their role change as a gain. One teacher leader commented, "The jury is still out on that one. I have lost my classroom, my students, and my place in the organization."

TLE stated, "I believe it is seen as a loss. Unless the culture within this building changes and begins to accept one of their colleagues helping them to be better teachers, most see my job as pointless." A couple of them put a more positive spin on this question. TLA commented, "It's a gain because I have learned more about my school, the departments, my colleagues, and the curriculum than I ever have before." TLB asserted, "I have been able to accomplish things for my department—initiatives that have been discussed for years but have never come to fruition due to time constraints."

Positive or Negative

Schlossberg (1981) states that oftentimes changes can produce both positive and negative feelings (p. 9). Similar to role change, any change involves some measure of stress. Similar to gain or loss, there was not a consensus regarding this transition as positive or negative. Interestingly, a few of the teachers mentioned trust in their answers. One teacher, who believed she had gained the trust of her colleagues, stated, "I see this as a neutral transition. Unless a teacher wants to change and sees a need for change, my job is at a standstill." TLB affirmed, "I am not sure the system trusts a position like this yet . . . they [teachers] still see me as a district person, not as a peer." TLA stated,

> It depends on the day. Some days I feel as though what I have done and am doing is so fulfilling and worthwhile. Other days, I feel as though I'm way out of my league, which is negative. I like to be in control, and often, my days feel out of control.

Duration

The expected duration of a transition is also a factor in adaptability (Schlossberg, 1981). Schlossberg argues, "Perhaps the greatest degree of stress and negative affect is connected with uncertainty" (p. 9). All of the teachers reported that there was a timeline associated with their new positions. Most stated that the duration for their current positions was between one to three years. Interestingly, all of them stated that they were told by the administration that they could return to the classroom when they wanted to.

TLD commented, "If after a year I wanted to go back to the classroom, I would be able to do so and that is still the case." It seemed that after spending five months in their current positions, at least a few of the teachers were ready to return to the classroom. TLE stated,

I have always said I will go back to the classroom. It is much easier to work with kids than adults. I love teaching and will definitely go back. I will not be doing this again next year . . . I plan to transition back to the classroom for the fall.

TLC stated, "I am uncertain at this point whether this is a permanent or temporary change. I am not sure right now."

Still Interested

Of the five teacher leaders, three responded that it is still too early to make a decision about continuing in their current roles next year. One of them commented,

I have always said that in order to do a job well it takes three years in order to get a good feel. However, there are days, I am ready to go back to the classroom in a heartbeat. Other days when I feel like I have made a difference, then I do not mind the job so much.

It was unfortunate to find out that TLE was already considering not continuing in her current role for next year. She stated, "I plan to plow through and do the best I can for the rest of this school year, but will bid into an upper elementary school classroom position for next year."

KEY TAKEAWAYS AND RECOMMENDATIONS

The search for affirmation is a recurring theme during this juncture in the five teacher leaders' journeys. In the "Pulse Check" portion of this chapter the reader was introduced to the idea of a teacher leadership evaluation process and what it might look like. It was recommended that this evaluation take elements of the PDP/PDR process, explained earlier, together with the Teacher Leader Model Standards, to produce a quality evaluation tool that can be adjusted to meet the needs of each teacher leader and district they are employed in.

The reason this evaluation tool was not introduced earlier, say the "Moving In" or early "Moving Through" period, is because not enough was known about the new role to create such an instrument. At this stage, five months into the new position, routines, duties, and work schedules had all, for the most part, been established for all five teacher leaders. TLA commented, "I no longer feel like I am trying to hit a moving target. I have a pretty good sense of where I am, what I need to, and where I need to be by this time."

The Teacher Leader Plan (TLP) should be developed by both the teacher leader and the administration together. The Teacher Leader Report (TLR)

will be completed at the end of the school year and it will be examined in greater depth in chapter 5. During the beginning stage of the TLP process, the teacher leader and administrator could and should go through each of the domains and the related goal areas to identify those that seem to mesh well with his or her current position. See appendix D (on page 105) for a full list of the standards and functions.

By utilizing Domain 1 Goal B as an example, hopefully it becomes clear that there are a variety of skills that could become a part of the TLP. The TLP for one teacher leader may look different from another teacher leader, and that is perfectly fine. The teacher leader and administrator would next predict or plan activities that are aligned to these skills. The skills have been bolded:

Goal B: *Models effective skills in **listening, presenting ideas, leading discussions, clarifying, mediating,** and **identifying the needs of self and others** in order to advance shared goals and professional learning.*

Potential activities aligned with these skills include:

- Listen to concerns from faculty members about a variety of topics. Act as an intermediary between faculty and administration.
- Present at staff meetings or PLC meetings.
- Plan and mediate follow-up meetings with faculty about new initiatives presented by administration or school board.
- Perform a needs assessment with all group of teachers, for example, English department, new faculty members, or community group.

The TLP document, similar to the Constitution, is meant to be a living and breathing document. There are some new measures that may emerge as the year progresses and that is perfectly fine. This last point should not be taken lightly. Some situations emerged for our new teacher leaders that they, and their administrators, did not see coming. It is imperative that these unforeseen events are noted in the teacher leader's daily journal. The hypothetical example described in the "Chapter Summary" section below is an example of a situation that occurred unexpectedly that would fit very nicely in Domain 1 Goal B.

The TLP example given shortly assesses only Domain 1. A similar document can be developed for the six remaining domains by using appendix D, which provides a detailed explanation of each domain and its related functions. Table 4.2 should be used as an organizational chart rather than the final document. The teacher leader can track his or her progress and jot down a few notes/dates on the table if he or she wishes. The TLR, on the other hand, should be a formal written document. It is recommended that the teacher

Table 4.2. TLP Domain 1

Rationale	Activity/Date	Evidence
Explain in detail why and how this will assist the teacher leader in his or her current position.	What specifically will the teacher leader do to satisfy this measure and when during the school year will these activities occur?	Explanation and supporting evidence.

Measures

Key phrases, areas of focus: Domain 1
- Adult Learning Theory
- Collegiality
- Continuous Improvement in Instruction
- Trust and Respect

Goals Associated with Domain 1

Goal A: Utilizes group processes to help colleagues work collaboratively to solve problems, make decisions, manage conflict, and promote meaningful change.

Goal B: Models effective skills in listening, presenting ideas, leading discussions, clarifying, mediating, and identifying the needs of self and others in order to advance shared goals and professional learning.

Goal C: Employs facilitation skills to create trust among colleagues, develop collective wisdom, and build ownership and action that supports student learning.

Goal D: Strives to create an inclusive culture where diverse perspectives are welcomed in addressing challenges.

Goal E: Uses knowledge and understanding of different backgrounds, ethnicities, cultures, and languages to promote effective interactions among colleagues.

leader use the TLP table in conjunction with a personal journal where he or she can write down his or her thoughts and ideas soon after the event.

Domain I: Fostering a Collaborative Culture to Support Educator
Development and Student Learning.

The teacher leader understands the principles of adult learning and knows how to develop a collaborative culture of collective responsibility in the school. The teacher leader uses this knowledge to promote an environment of collegiality, trust, and respect that focuses on continuous improvement in instruction and student learning.

CHAPTER SUMMARY

The overarching themes for this late "Moving Through" stage were the search for affirmation and managing some of the nuances of the new role that were causing stress for the new teacher leaders. As stated previously, feeling as though you are doing quality work and knowing that you are doing quality work are two totally different things. It would be hard for anyone so new in his or her position to know for certain that he or she is satisfying all of the requirements and all of the needs of those individuals he or she is working with.

Most of the teacher leaders did state that they had received very favorable comments from their administrators, but these positive comments were not sufficient. Some of the leaders commented on the amount of stress and anxiety they are still feeling as the year progresses. There are two things that can be a saving grace at this latter "Moving Through" phase for new teacher leaders. One is to take care of yourself outside of the school setting to deal with the stress. The other is to continue journaling and recording your experiences on your TLP.

In my previous role as a PK–12 administrator I would tell the new teachers that people who work in educational settings are people professionals. People professionals learn how to take care of themselves when they are not on the job and fill up their "reserve tank," for lack of a better term. Too often we find ourselves pulled in so many different directions during the day and doing things for other people that we neglect our own needs. People professionals find a way to unwind and replenish their "reserve tank" that on some days is near empty by mid-day.

People professionals make sure to have their reserve tanks full when they walk through the schoolhouse doors by doing things that they find rewarding outside of work. Some listen to music, others spend time with their families,

Table 4.3.   Journaling Example

Measures	Activity/Date	Evidence
	What specifically will the teacher leader do to satisfy this measure and when during the school year will these activities occur?	*Explanation and supporting evidence.*
Goal B: Models effective skills in **listening, presenting ideas, leading discussions, clarifying, mediating,** and **identifying the needs of self and others** in order to advance shared goals and professional learning.	**Chair of English Department asked me to attend their next department meeting.** **Listening: 1/10** Met with English Department about concerns they have with goal-setting procedure given to them by administration. **Leading Discussion: 1/19** Met with English Department and clarified the goal-setting procedure as seen through the administrative lens. Clarified that the administration will allow the department to establish two goals and choose two goals from a list of five goals set by administration. English Department members responded favorably to goal-setting procedure and discussion was had about possible goals and when the next meeting should be scheduled.	**1/10** Notes taken during English Department meeting. **1/11** Scheduled meeting with Principal Jones to express concerns and offer possible solutions. Scheduled new meeting with English Department. **1/19** Notes taken during English Department meeting. **1/21** Follow-up meeting with Principal Jones about favorable English Department meeting results.

others work out. The trick is to find yours and dedicate the time necessary to have a full tank at the beginning of the day.

Self-Reflection

• What is it that you do outside of the workplace to replenish your "reserve tank?"

Journaling and documenting experiences on the TDP should help reassure new teacher leaders that they are making progress in achieving their goals, and honestly, making progress might be all that can be determined at this juncture. Let's revisit Domain 1 Goal B as a point of reference that emphasizes the importance of journaling. The rationale column has been eliminated for our purposes here.

In this hypothetical situation, the teacher leader finds himself meeting with the English Department chair to discuss the PLC goal-setting procedure set forth by the administration. After careful analysis, many of the skills outlined in Domain 1 Goal B have been experienced and documented. These experiences, documented on the TLP and included in the personal journal, can now become a part of the TLR.

One of the "Self-Reflection" questions at the beginning of this chapter was:

• Were there times in previous jobs when you thought you couldn't endure but continued to soldier on? What was it that you did that pushed you past the difficult times?

Two potential answers to this question are to take care of yourself outside of the school setting and continue to journal and record your experiences on your TLP.

Chapter 5

Moving Out

Planning for the Future

The internal mindset of individuals about leadership ability, or their leadership mindset, is a critical component related to their effectiveness and success as a leader.

—Chase, 2010, p. 297

The information contained in both chapters 5 and 6 will be taken from the fourth and final interview that occurred in late May. The focus for chapter 5 will be on the concluding thoughts of the participants as they relate to some of the factors specifically concentrating on Situation. Chapter 6 will deliberate on how the teacher leaders perceived their growth in leadership capacity and also their development in the explicit teacher leadership skills outlined in chapter 2.

The beginning of this chapter offers an opportunity to revisit something from the introduction that is also relevant to the "Moving Out" stage. This significance became apparent after analyzing the results from the fourth and final interview. One of the main themes that was identified during the last interview was mindset. This naturally led to ruminations about growth mindset and fixed mindset popularized by Carol Dweck (2006).

Not to let the cat out of the bag, but it became very apparent that those teacher leaders who were more confident and positive at the end of the year were exhibiting some of the same characteristics that are assigned to a growth mindset. On the flipside, those who were ending their first year on an unenthusiastic note and seemed quite pessimistic were displaying dispositions more aligned to a fixed mindset. This revelation led me to reflect on something written about in the introduction, the four dispositions of quality teacher leaders. A short summary of each is given below.

Teacher Leaders Have Initiative—Teacher leaders do not wait for permission to do what they know is good for their school and their students. Teacher leaders do not need administrative directives to know and understand what their school, their colleagues, and their students require to be successful. Having initiative is not enough. Teacher leaders are also creative, resourceful, and good planners. A key feature of this disposition is being persistent and sticking with something even though it is not going as planned.

Teacher Leaders Are Assertive—A big part of being assertive is having confidence that your motives and goals are attainable. This confidence might come from prior achievements or quite possibly this is the first time you have been passionate enough about something that you have decided to "put yourself out there," so to speak, and operate outside your comfort zone.

Teacher Leaders Are Invested—In my experience, most teacher leaders have at least three years of classroom teaching experience under their belts. As you have read in chapter 2, the relationships you once had with your colleagues will change once you move into any type of leadership position at your school. If your colleagues see you as too different it will be more difficult for you to establish a trusting relationship with them. Teacher leaders actually seek out and build relationships with people who will challenge them.

A Teacher Leader Understands Adult Learning Theory—Depending on what it is that you are asked to do in your new role, you might be setting expectations for your colleagues, asking them to complete certain tasks in a timely manner, and having them demonstrate to you that they understand and can apply certain topics that you have discussed with them. Teacher leaders have a passion for learning about topics, like Adult Learning Theory, that they know little about.

These dispositions (assertive, initiative, and vested) and knowledge of Adult Learning Theory ally quite nicely with a growth mindset. A person with a fixed mindset would view leadership as an innate quality or believe that people are born leaders. A person with a growth mindset would believe that leadership abilities can be learned and acquired through effort and experience (Dweck, 2006). This topic will be examined in greater detail in the "Key Takeaways and Recommendations" section of this chapter.

PULSE CHECK

One of the best things about the "Moving Out" stage for the researcher is that no question was off the table. No matter the subject, more often than not the teacher leaders had, after a calendar school year, an experience that corresponded to the questions asked. The dilemma for the researcher is to make certain that the right questions are asked. Should the focus at this stage be on Situation and Self? Should the focus be on Strategies and Support? After careful deliberation, it was decided that the emphasis for the final interview would focus primarily on Situation, specifically the topics of gain/loss, positive/negative, and degree of stress.

The reason for doing so is quite simple. The apprehension and angst that the teacher leader might have been experiencing at the latter part of the "Moving Through" stage (late January, early February) would hopefully be diminished by the end of the school year. It was anticipated that a more accurate picture of how the teacher leaders were feeling, in relation to the factors discussed earlier, could be determined when the stressors associated with the job were no longer there.

For example, one teacher leader made the following statement regarding positive or negative change in her third interview during the late "Moving Through" Stage. TLB stated, "I'm coming off a tough week for me . . . last Thursday, I was ready to quit." That same teacher leader made the following comment in interview four during the "Moving Out" stage: "I am finding out that people need more guidance. I've worked hard on relationship building and was pleased when some of the teachers started to apply some of my suggestions to their teaching." What a difference a few months make.

At this stage of the research there were quite a few generalizations that could be made about the five teacher leaders who participated in this study in regard to Self and Support. Strategies was not much of a focus for the fourth interview nor in this chapter because it was examined in great detail in the previous chapter. There were still some questions about Situation that needed to be answered before the research was concluded.

By the "Moving Out" stage, regarding Self, a few generalizations can be made about our five teacher leaders:

- *Strengths/Weaknesses*: A major strength was longevity (number of years in the district) and with that came a clear understanding of the culture of the school they worked at. Understandably, the teachers mentioned weaknesses more often in their responses. Many reported that they had learned to be more assertive, that integrity and ethos became pillars upon which they depended daily, and that they realized the value of confidentiality above all else. Even though all of the teacher leaders had worked with their colleagues in various capacities in the past, their greatest weakness was grasping the nuances associated with working with adults on a daily basis.
- *Balance*: Finding a balance, or not, was mentioned by most of the teacher leaders. Balance was often associated with time and adapting to various situations that needed immediate attention. TLA shared during the "Moving

Through" stage, "I have developed a pretty good system where I have all my meetings, observations, and tasks written down on my weekly calendar. I have learned to schedule [free time] to handle unanticipated events." An important point here is that balance, as it relates to time/task distribution, will only become a reality in the latter part of the "Moving Through" stage.

By the "Moving Out" stage, there were some generalizations that could be made about Support that our teacher leaders experienced as well. A recurring theme for all of the teacher leaders was that it is difficult to support a position that is constantly evolving. TLC stated, "My principal has been great. He supports me with basically whatever it is that I need." TLD maintained, "I've needed to wrap my head around the fact that I am the one who informs the principal what types of supports I need. Early on, I thought this was something that was planned for."

Spouse and Co-Workers

No question, the greatest source of support for the teacher leaders was their spouses. TLE stated,

> There are things I can talk about with my husband that I can't discuss with anyone else. I like the fact that I can be unprofessional and vent about things that are happening that I know nothing about. It's therapeutic, in a sense.

This was a way for the teacher leaders to fill up their reserve tank for the next day. TLB argued, "Because my husband is so far removed from what I am experiencing, it was nice to hear his perspective on various topics and issues. This [venting] allowed me to see things in a different light."

Second to spousal support were the other teacher leaders that were in the building or in the district. As was stated in an earlier chapter, one school had two new teacher leaders, TLA and TLB, going through the experience together. These two leaned on each other quite often throughout the year. TLA asserted,

> Sometimes I would have a bad experience and in talking about it with TLB, I found that she had a similar experience but approached it differently and it went just fine. Taking her suggestions to heart made me look forward to a similar experience rather than dread it.

Self-Reflection

• If you don't have another teacher leader in your school or district experiencing this transition at the same time that you are, what tools or strategies are at your disposal to communicate with a new teacher leader in a neighboring district?

RESEARCH QUESTIONS AND
EXPLANATION OF FINDINGS

Gain or Loss?

The topic of evaluation was discussed at great length in chapter 4. For all of the five teacher leaders there was not a formal evaluation structure in place that resembled the TLP/TLR process. This begs the question, is it fair to ask the teacher leaders whether they see this experience as a gain or a loss without an evaluation tool? On the flipside, if there were an evaluation structure in place, by the "Moving Out" stage the new teacher leaders could simply reflect on the measure, rationale, activities, and measurement portion of their TLP and determine which of these tasks had been completed and which had not. This same type of evaluation could be performed by an analysis of their personal goals and the progress that was made on each.

In the few months since the same questions about gain or loss were asked during interview three, it is safe to state that there was a definite shift in opinion for all of the teacher leaders. For one of the five teacher leaders, TLE, she decided that it would be in her best interest to return to the classroom. She stated, "It has been a gain for the system and the grade level, but a loss for me personally. I am certain that I will not be doing this again next year and I plan to transition back into the classroom for the fall." For the rest of the teacher leaders, they all plan to stay in their current positions for the following year.

During the last interview, TLB asserted, "I miss my kids and I miss being in the classroom. When I read about new strategies and things I get excited because I want to try that. I don't have a classroom of kids so it kind of depends on what you are talking about." In stark contrast, TLA, when asked about whether the transition has been a gain or a loss, responded, "We are getting things a little more organized in our department, so that is definitely a gain." I couldn't help but notice the use of the words "I" and "we" in many of the responses. This revelation led to the discovery of one of the major themes during interview four in regard to loss/gain and positive/negative, that being "systems thinking."

In layman's terms, a system is a group or combination of parts that form a complex or unitary whole. Every system has a purpose, and in the case of teacher leadership, that purpose is to assist in improving student achievement. The teacher leadership system definitely has a purpose and has the opportunity to create value. Couched within each system are processes. Processes are all the related activities (parts) inside the system that work together to make it function. It's important that processes (practices to assist teacher leaders in this case) are effective so that the system can run efficiently. Those teacher leaders, who at the end of the year came to an understanding that certain processes were not working as well as they should during the first year, perceived the transition as a gain.

TLA made the following comment during the last interview:

> The more I read the research about teacher leadership, I think we have good instincts with what we have implemented and see some of what we are doing in the research. It would have been nice to have it in reverse, but maybe that is the charm of it too. This organic process of finding things out like that using our instincts to find the right course of action.

TLC stated:

> I think the process had to evolve. The first thing is to figure out what we are and what we do and get the teachers comfortable. The next step is to get the teachers content with this process. I think we really need to work on some type of self-reflection piece with the teachers . . . give the teachers a voice, so to speak, in how we go about our business.

TLB claimed, "We have some good things in place for our department moving forward . . . credit recovery has gotten started and we have made progress with our program No Red Ink. The department is getting things a little more organized."

Positive or Negative

Systems thinking naturally spilled into the questions about whether the transition is seen as a positive move or a negative move as well. Not all teacher leaders viewed their experience as a positive by the fourth interview, but most did. TLA spoke at great length about her positive experience:

> I see this as a positive . . . not sure when this happened, but some time in my life I have started to see obstacles as opportunities and I like to problem solve. Yes, there have been negatives too, but overall it has been positive.

TLB commented similarly:

> One positive is getting way more educated about how this entire school works. I didn't know much about English Language Learners [ELL] before this and also Special Education [SPED]. I didn't really understand them and

my perspective. I have a better understanding of where they are going and what they want to accomplish. I think I have been living in a bubble for the last twenty years or so.

TLB spoke directly to the ELL and SPED staff in her response. She indicated that this was a major positive that came out of her experiences during the first year. She asserted:

I think they [SPED and ELL] are thankful for the attention we have been giving them. They have been flying solo for so many years. I believe we have helped them have a more linear system that provides them with direction.

TLC spoke directly to "systems" in her statement:

We exist to increase student achievement. . . . I feel as though I have been making good forward motion in setting up systems and building relationships to try to make that [student achievement] happen. We want this change to happen now, but this is a new system and this is the suspicion year and sometimes we take negative reactions personally. As much as I get frustrated, I am going to stick it out for another year. I did too much work to allow someone else to come in and take over.

TLE made specific comments during this final interview that sounded like a person at the end of her rope. In response to the negatives associated with her role, she stated,

The behavior of certain adults has been the most challenging, devastating, and eye-opening experience. I have been floored by some of the disrespect, entitlements, and rudeness that has come with some of my work. I have been continually heartbroken by the amount of educators I have seen who are looking for short-cuts, or solutions that meet their own needs and not necessarily the needs of their students.

Degree of Stress

It is important to reiterate something that was stated early in this chapter. It was anticipated that the degree of stress the teacher leaders felt in early February (third interview) would be greater than what they experienced when the school year was winding down in May (fourth interview).

TLC made the following comment in her answer about the degree of stress: "I feel that it is higher mainly because I've learned to be patient with this job. A lot has to happen before decisions have to be made." TLB commented similarly about the level of stress:

There is stress, but a different type of stress. In this position I feel the stress to feel smart. I don't feel smart a lot of the time and I think I need to get to a Zen-like state to really think things through all the way to the end, yet there are all these tasks that need to be completed.

TLD also spoke to the importance of time management and finding time to think while performing this job. He stated:

The interruptions can be frustrating and I believe I need some really good thinking time. I believe I have good instincts when it comes to problem solving, if I can think all the way through the issue. I simply need to shut the door and process.

KEY TAKEAWAYS AND RECOMMENDATIONS

The idea of having a growth versus a fixed mindset was introduced at the beginning of this chapter and will be examined in greater detail here using Dweck's explanations of characteristics assigned to each. The format for this examination will proceed as follows:

• Statement about fixed mindset compared to growth mindset in connection to a specific characteristic as defined by Dweck.
• Samples from teacher leader interviews that are aligned with each mindset.
• Recommendations for teacher leaders moving into their second year.

Qualities

Those with a fixed mindset believe that their basic qualities or traits are fixed and unchangeable. Those with a growth mindset believe that their basic qualities can and should be nurtured and that everyone can change through application and experience (Dweck, 2006). A few of the fundamental qualities teacher leaders possess were described at the beginning of this chapter. These were initiative, assertive, and invested.

Those with a fixed mindset more often than not cited a lack of training and experience for their deficiencies or lack of progress in working with their teachers. Those teacher leaders with a growth mindset pressed through their lack of training and from their experiences working with teachers and reflecting on those experiences developed their own way of managing challenging situations.

TLA made the following comment during the last interview in which she acknowledged her lack of training but also her maturity in having conversations with the teachers she is working with. She stated:

I would have liked to have known the communication process as far as when you have conversations with teachers. . . . I would have liked to see that earlier. The post observation conversation . . . when you cross the border from how was your kid's basketball game to okay . . . you know, let's get down to business. I feel like I am still feeling around in the dark and am not very efficient with conversations like that, but I am much better than I was at the beginning of the year.

TLD made a similar comment in regard to his growth in conversing with the teachers he is working with:

I feel like early on, I dictated the conversation when I should be listening more. But I think it is new for everyone. . . . I had two great conversations last Friday . . . then I thought to myself . . . ohh . . . did I listen well enough? Did I really hear what they said? I think both the teacher and myself are more used to the conversations, but I need to listen better.

A common theme uttered throughout this segment was the importance of experience and reflection. Most authors reference John Dewey, who is mentioned in chapter 2, when the topic of experience and understanding by doing is brought up in educational circles. The experiential nature of the transition from classroom teacher to teacher leader in these cases lends itself more to the work of David and Alice Kolb. David Kolb's Experiential Learning Theory (ELT) consists of four dimensions: concrete experience, reflective observation, abstract conceptualization, and active experimentation. These four dimensions are essential for the learner, or teacher leader in this case, to gain knowledge and ultimately to learn from experience (Kolb, 1984).

Kolb's model focuses on the importance of reflection in the learning process and the cyclical nature of Kolb's model facilitates the integration of the direct learning experience and abstract generalization, with reflection as the linking function.

The ELT model portrays two dialectically related modes of grasping experience—concrete experience and abstract conceptualization—and two dialectically related modes of transforming experience—reflective observation and active experimentation. Experiential learning is a process of constructing knowledge that involves a creative tension among the four learning modes that is responsive to contextual demands. This process is portrayed as an idealized learning cycle or spiral in which the learner "touches all the bases" experiencing, reflecting, thinking, and acting—in a recursive process that is responsive to the learning situation and what is being learned" (Kolb & Kolb, 2005, p. 194).

This is good counsel for any new teacher leader in his or her first year. The dispositions you possess early on can and will be cultivated through

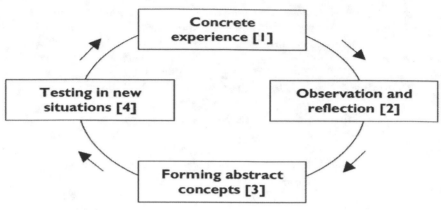

Figure 5.1. Kolb's Experiential Learning Model

your experiences working with the classroom teachers in your building. In chapter 2 the importance of keeping a reflective journal was presented. Your journaling exercises will serve you well in your journey through experience, reflection, thinking, and application.

Teacher or Teacher Leader?

One of the simplest ways to ascertain a fixed or a growth mindset during the final interview was to discern how the teacher leaders referred to themselves. Those with a fixed mindset still depicted themselves as a teacher or utilized techniques that worked well in the classroom but not so well in a leadership position. Those with a growth mindset thought of themselves as a colleague but also acknowledged that they are now working with adults and not students.

Fortunately almost all of the teacher leaders, by the end of the school year, had acknowledged that their position was different from that of the teachers they were working with. TLC, in one of her answers about working with teachers, made the following comment: "At first I thought I could model how I teach . . . if I could show it, then I thought I could actually help teachers teach better." TLC also made the following comment that illustrated her understanding that modeling might not work as well as she thought:

> I walk the fine balance between them coming to you and asking for help and you work out a system. I am finding out that the teachers need more guidance . . . I have a good enough relationship where they would try some of my suggestions and we can talk about what went well and what didn't . . . but with some teachers, maybe I need to go in the direction of point blank . . . here is what you need to do. I am still trying it out as I go . . . not trying too hard too fast.

TLA compared her new role to that of a teacher. "Teaching was easier . . . this is new . . . I get really tired thinking about all the little details. I feel a lot like a first year teacher . . . trying to get the system down."

It was interesting to listen to some of the teacher leaders discuss their new roles and how appreciative their administrator was for their insight on matters that in the past had been done solely by the administration. TLA made the following comment:

> Even in regard to the systems we have had in place . . . like ELL . . . I have looked at restructuring models from a teacher's standpoint . . . he listens to my teacher perspective on it and he gives the administrative perspective. He said, it is time to look at things from a different perspective now . . . he values our feedback . . . we are part of the system . . . I do have a say . . . he values our input.

TLB spoke directly to her new role in her statement:

> We do still see things from a teacher's point of view . . . liaison or bridge . . . from the teacher's world. We didn't know as much as we do now about the school system . . . there is the center and the spokes to the outer wheel and a part of our job is to make sure we are all working together.

Transitioning into a different role is never an easy thing to do. M. Scott Peck famously stated:

> The truth is that our finest moments are most likely to occur when we are feeling deeply uncomfortable, unhappy, or unfulfilled. For it is only in such moments, propelled by our discomfort, that we are likely to step out of our ruts and start searching for different ways or truer answers. (quoted in Johnson, 2018)

Through their experiences almost all of the teacher leaders discovered that in order to move forward, they needed to begin thinking like a leader rather than as a teacher. They were still part of the system, but the process and manner in which they went about their day-to-day activities were much different than they were a year ago.

CHAPTER SUMMARY

In chapter 1 a comment was made about the "Moving Out" stage that it does not mark the transition to a new role or position but rather a move away from a position being so new and uncertain. In a perfect world a follow-up interview could have been done during the summer months to discern what was learned during the first year in their new roles, and, more importantly, how these new teacher leaders will use their experiences to better prepare for the next school year. Obviously, that did not happen.

The "Moving Out" stage does mark the end of our analysis of the Four Ss. But it does beg the question, which of the factors will continue to be a consideration over the summer months and into next year? Take some time to deliberate on these questions prior to moving on to the final chapter that focuses on leadership skills and development.

- What are specific "wide-ranging" factors that merit further deliberation over the summer as you begin planning for year two? List a few ideas, techniques, or processes you have learned along the way that will allow you to use your experiences to be primed for year two.
- Now that you know a little more about the ELT, think about specific situations where you have used Kolb's ELT Model this past year without even knowing it. How can you intentionally utilize this model as you prepare for your second year?

Table 5.1.   Interview #4

Factors	Moving Out (MO) Late May
Situation	
New Role	X
Positive or Negative?	X
Gain or Loss?	X
Self	
Strengths/Weaknesses	X
Support	
Co-Workers	X
Spouse	X
Strategies—Coping	
Balance/Flexibility	X

Chapter 6

Perceptions of Leadership Growth

As stated in the introduction, chapter 6 will be written a little differently from the past four chapters. The five teacher leaders have completed their first year and some are now beginning their "Moving In" stage for the next school year. Throughout this journey with these new teacher leaders it was important to design the research questions for the first three interviews that aligned closely with Schlossberg's transition theory, the Four Ss, and the concepts of "Moving In, Through, and Out." Chapter 6 is different.

The primary focus for the last interview was twofold. First, to complete the analysis of the three stages and the Four Ss and related factors. This was completed and detailed in chapter 5. Second, the final interview was intentionally designed to scrutinize leadership growth. There are two parts to this leadership inquiry. The first part will focus primarily on how the teacher leaders perceived themselves growing in their leadership capacity. The second part will involve an analysis into how the five teacher leaders have developed the explicit teacher leadership skills that were mentioned in chapter 2. The questions asked during the last interview included those listed here:

- What do you wish you would have known about your position?
- How have you grown as a leader?

For convenience sake, here are the ten skills that were listed and examined in chapter 2. The *italicized* skills are those that were mentioned directly or indirectly by the teacher leaders during the last interview:

- *Communication*
- *Listening/Collaboration*

- Adult Learning Theory
- Organization
- Facilitation
- Reflection
- Research (Action Research)
- Modeling
- *Big Picture Thinking/Philosophy*
- *Advocacy*

The teacher responses were transcribed, as usual, but these ten leadership skills provided the framework or structure for the analysis of the fourth interview rather than Schlossberg's theory or the Four Ss. That being said, the final interview and the questions were designed without the encumbrances of "sticking to the script."

This freedom allowed the researcher to ask questions that could only be answered by someone who has experienced the trials and tribulations of a first-year teacher leader. Anyone who has performed qualitative research can appreciate that the informal, conversational, open-ended questions oftentimes produce the sweetest fruit, and this analysis was no different.

PART ONE: LEADERSHIP INQUIRY

The overarching themes that were uncovered during the first part of the analysis included authenticity and servant leadership along with elements of communication, listening, big picture philosophy, and advocacy. In the introduction it was stated that teacher leaders possess certain dispositions like assertiveness, initiative, are invested in their institution, and have a good working knowledge of Adult Learning Theory. Add to this list of dispositions the ten skills documented earlier and it might be easy to understand how leadership has somehow been pushed aside by supposedly more pressing matters.

When asked the question about how they had grown as a leader, TLA stated, "Yikes, I don't think you can ask me that question. You should probably ask those that I have been working with for the past year." What a great answer. Quite possibly, humility should be added to the list of dispositions discussed earlier. One of the things that struck me after I asked this question was how long it took each of the participants to answer. It was almost as if the term "leadership" wasn't even on their radar. It was somehow washed away in the minutiae of what they had been doing for the entire year.

Teacher leadership, rooted into the culture of a school, might appear ambivalent or reticent, but it is there. One just needs to dig a little deeper to uncover instances in which teacher leaders are influencing those they are working with. One needs to dig a little deeper to find examples where the classroom teachers that they are supporting are working toward or achieving their personal or classroom goals and maximizing their efforts. Only after careful analysis did it become clear that the way some of these new teacher leaders influenced those they were working with was by them being authentic. Couched within this definition of authenticity are evidences of trust, being realistic, and reliability.

TLB stated,

> I would say . . . I had personal integrity before this year, but it has grown a little more now . . . I don't have the opportunity to commiserate any longer . . . making comments about another teacher with my colleagues . . . I have distanced myself from it to maintain my personal integrity with those I am now working with.

TLA asserted,

> I want to work with everybody and I don't want anyone to think that I have preconceived notions about them. I want them to feel comfortable with me . . . to understand that our conversations will be kept private . . . this is very important to me and I have found that it is probably more important for them.

TLE suggested,

> After working with a group of teachers the entire year, they have come to rely on me to give them the straight scoop about some of the decisions or initiatives that have been made by the department chair or administration. I can talk to them using "teacher speak," putting it in terms that they comprehend and explain what this means for them.

TLD echoed these sentiments when he stated,

> My part of it is the extra knowledge I have gained. . . . I have developed a wider perspective looking at things from everyone's point of view . . . district office, principal, math department. I need to know the Big Picture before I can make certain decisions or pass on certain information.

This is a nice segue into Big Picture, one of the ten skills listed earlier. Coquyt and Creasman (2017) explain the Big Picture philosophy as follows:

> Teacher leaders, like all great leaders, realize that the positon is much bigger than the individual who holds the position. They understand that their success is determined by their effectiveness in serving and empowering others and growing a culture that is conducive to shared, distributed and collaborative leadership.

Teacher leaders see the big picture past their position and role, to exactly how they can help others and assist in leading school transformation. Too often, leaders are only leaders in title, but fail to accept the awesome responsibility that the position brings with it. Many fall victim to the position. To be successful, teacher leaders must remain focused on the work, the big picture of ensuring that students succeed. (p. 111)

TLB made the following comments that summarize her Big Picture philosophy quite nicely:

From the teacher's point of view it is always we want we want we want kind of deal. At the same time I know the reason why administration has to say no now and again. I get to share this perspective with the teachers . . . I didn't have this knowledge or this perspective before. Hopefully, just the knowledge I am gaining . . . the overall spectrum . . . I have a better understanding of how the system works. At first I thought I would be the voice for the math department in this position . . . sometimes I have to agree with the other side and say "here's why."

Elements of servant leadership were also detected in a few of the responses from the final interview. Coquyt and Creasman (2017) describe servant leadership as follows:

Servant leadership is based on the premise that leaders who are best able to motivate followers are those who focus least on satisfying their own personal needs and most on prioritizing the fulfillment of followers' needs (Greenleaf, 1998). Leaders who are more concerned about others than themselves are humble, and their humility stimulates strong relationships with followers and encourages followers to become fully engaged in their work. (p. 69)

TLA actually mentioned servant leadership in one of her responses. She stated,

The teachers in the communications department do come to me with their needs . . . some call me their boss . . . this could be because I was the department chair. I try to look at things from their perspective . . . kind of a servant leadership type thing. . . . I am better able to explain [why] to my colleagues now and help them work out a plan to get at least some of their needs met.

TLE indicated that attending to the needs of adults in her current position was a far cry from attending to the needs of the students in her classroom a year ago. She stated,

Through the use of formative assessments it was actually quite simple to determine the strengths and weaknesses of your students when you are teaching a particular skill or covering a unit of study. Some of them required one on one instruction and some only required minimal scaffolding in order to get them to the next level. If you don't meet with your teachers on a daily basis, some maybe only once a week, their needs have a tendency to pile up.

TLC also mentioned working with adults in one of her responses. She stated,

> First of all, I need to be very respectful when I am working through an issue with one of the classroom teachers. I understand where they are coming from because I have been in their position for a number of years. I need to craft my responses in a way that flips the responsibility to solve this issue on them, if that makes sense. My ultimate goal is to have them leave our meeting with relevant and practical strategies that they can use the next time they encounter this problem.

It was satisfying to hear about how each of the new teacher leaders explained their growth as a leader in their respective schools. Once again, what was very interesting is that even though they were exercising true leadership, few of the teacher leaders realized it until after the interview was over. Quite possibly, this leadership reflection could be included in the personal journal entries that should be completed on a weekly basis.

PART TWO: TEACHER LEADERSHIP SKILLS INQUIRY

The second part of this analysis revolved around the ten teacher leadership skills that were mentioned at the beginning of this chapter. It is important to keep in mind that just because a skill is listed as essential doesn't mean it needs to be mastered by the end of the first year. Honestly, the mere mention of one of the ten skills was what I was hoping for in the final interview. If one or another teacher leader mentioned a skill, it insinuated that it was at least on their radar and I was satisfied with that.

Before launching into the examination of the ten teacher leadership skills, please perform the self-reflection activity below.

Self-Reflection

- Think about a skill or disposition that is essential for you to master in your current position. What have you done to mature from novice to master as it relates to this particular skill?
- How long did it take to master that particular skill? Are you still somewhere between novice and master?
- In your estimation, can this particular skill be mastered or is it something that is constantly evolving and developing?

This self-reflection exercise should help put things into perspective as it relates to skill development for any position. Real-world experiences provide the best opportunities to develop any skill, and that includes the teacher leadership skills sprinkled throughout this chapter. Once again, Kolb's ELT Model could prove to be useful for the reflective processes that should occur shortly after experiencing something new or different. The ten teacher leader skills could perhaps provide a reflective backdrop to ensure that they are at least considered after every new experience.

I spent over ten years as a high school principal and can honestly state that there are skills associated with the position that were never mastered; the skills were honed, maybe, but never mastered. It took quite a few years to be experienced enough to walk into a classroom and "know what I was seeing versus seeing what I know" in regard to quality teaching. Needless to say, I was a long way from mastering the skills needed to develop quality teachers.

For simplicity's sake, the *italicized* skills listed alongside the research questions below specify which teacher leader skill was discovered or identified during the analysis of the specific teacher leadership skills included in that question.

What Do You Wish You Would Have Known? *Communication, Listening, Collaboration, Adult Learning*

Almost to a person, the unanimous answer to this question, "What do you wish you would have known?" was related in some way to working with adults. Couched within their answers was communication, more specifically face-to-face communication. Both working with adults or knowledge of Adult Learning Theory and Communication were previously discussed in chapter 2 as essential teacher leadership skills. TLD stated, "Working with adults is a whole different ballgame than working with kids. It's a different set of kid gloves that you wear." TLB echoed this sentiment when she stated, "I wish I would have known that I would not know how to do this."

There were a few specifics that could be discerned when asked probing questions explicitly about what it was that was difficult. One specific area was simply having conversations with classroom teachers. TLC asserted, "I used to have conversations with these people all the time and it felt perfectly natural." When urged to explain what was unnatural, she stated, "They look at me as different from them now, like I have some sort of authority or something. I feel like this is very odd, to still have these feelings at the end of the year."

TLA has a similar reply when asked about the difficulty having meaningful conversations with classroom teachers. She asserted,

> It is very difficult to move the needle with an adult. I always felt comfortable that I could move my students in the direction I wanted when I was in the

classroom. To try to move the needle with an adult, now that is different. I keep asking myself, when do you get pushy, when do you get bitchy, when are you starting to cross the line versus encouraging them?

Keeping with the difficult conversations theme, TLD offered,

> I have been in situations where I know there are deficiencies in their teaching, based on my experiences, and I have difficulty handling the transition from what went well to what needs a little more work. I would love it if they would come right out and say, "this part of the lesson didn't go as well as it could have" but that has only happened on a few occasions.

Not everything was a struggle though. One teacher leader felt like she was past feeling uncomfortable with the conversations and started to identify things that she could do that might make future conversations more bearable. TLA asserted,

> I feel like I am listening more and talking a whole lot less. I also take a lot of notes during our conversations. After our conversation, I can look over my notes, like you do, and find things that I may have missed during our conversation. I also share my notes with the teacher so they don't think anything sneaky is going on.

Being an active listener and quality communicator is easier said than done. Domain 1, Function B from the Teacher Leader Model Standards states, "The teacher leader models effective skills in listening, presenting ideas, leading discussions, clarifying, mediating, and identifying the needs of self and others in order to advance shared goals and professional learning" (Creasman & Coquyt, 2016, p. 9). The authors also contend,

> Teacher leaders must be good listeners who are accessible. Fellow teachers respect and hold teacher leaders in high regard and expect them to be sounding boards for ideas and advocates for their departments as well as for teachers. Teacher leaders are able to garner support and have everyone working toward the same goals, as a result of their ability to communicate effectively. (p. 10)

Self-Reflection

It would be useful at this point for the teacher leader to reflect on what was examined from chapter 2 in regard to communication, collaboration/listening, and Adult Learning Theory. The tables have been altered a bit in order to measure growth in each skill. A comparison of the answers from chapter 2 to the present time should provide the reader with an indication of how they have grown in each of the skills presented here.

Table 6.1. Communication Skills

Rate How Capable You Are with the Following Teacher Leader Skill
(4) *Very Capable* (3) *Capable* (2) *Somewhat Capable* (1) *Not Capable at All*

Communication	4	3	2	1

Based on your experiences throughout the year, a) explain how you have strengthened this skill and b) how might you continue to build upon your communication skills, specifically during face-to-face communication?

Where do you rate yourself now as compared to your rating from earlier in the year? Besides experience, is there anything else that can account for this change?

Table 6.2. Listening/Collaboration Skills

Rate How Capable You Are with the Following Teacher Leader Skill
(4) *Very Capable* (3) *Capable* (2) *Somewhat Capable* (1) *Not Capable at All*

Listening/Collaboration	4	3	2	1

Based on your experiences throughout the year, a) explain how you have strengthened this skill and b) how might you continue to build upon your listening skills, specifically during face-to-face conversations?

If this skill is still considered a growth area (1 or 2), what can you do right now to improve your proficiency?

Table 6.3. Adult Learning Skills

Rate How Capable You Are with the Following Teacher Leader Skill
(4) *Very Capable* (3) *Capable* (2) *Somewhat Capable* (1) *Not Capable at All*

Adult Learning Theory	4	3	2	1

Based on your experiences throughout the year, a) explain how you have strengthened this skill and b) how might you continue to build upon your understanding of working with adults and Adult Learning Theory?

Where do you rate yourself now as compared to your rating from earlier in the year? Besides experience, is there anything else that can account for this change?

HOW HAVE YOU GROWN AS A LEADER?

This was no doubt one of the most important questions that was posed at the end of the school year. It was stated earlier that the latter part of chapter 2 examined in detail many of the basic skills teacher leaders must possess. Three of those skills (communication, listening/advocacy, and Adult Learning Theory) were mentioned by most of the participants in response to the first interview question and were examined earlier. It is safe to state that these specific skills could and should be examined and researched at great length during the "Moving In" stage for a first-year teacher leader.

The fact that the skills were just mentioned, in my estimation, was a very good result for a couple of reasons. It proved that without consciously being aware, many of the participants were analyzing and testing their proficiency with some of the leadership skills up to the end of the first year. Secondly, it demonstrated that none of the ten teacher leadership skills were mastered at the end of the first year. Some were attended to more than others (see earlier discussion) and some were barely mentioned at all.

To reiterate, the following remaining skills were also cited in chapter 2 as essential for teacher leaders to possess and continue to refine and develop. The skills Big Picture and advocacy were examined in part one of this chapter and will not be explored any further.

- Organization
- Facilitation
- Reflection
- Research (Action Research)
- Modeling
- Big Picture
- Advocacy

It may be simpler to begin by listing those leadership skills that weren't mentioned in any of the responses from the fourth interview, followed by those skills that were mentioned by one or maybe two of the participants. It should be pointed out that just because they weren't mentioned does not mean that these skills were pushed aside or deemed not important by the participants. It simply means that they weren't stated in the responses and did not merit any further investigation here. It would have been easier to mention each skill in the questions asked by the researcher, but obviously this would fly in the face of true qualitative investigation.

Organization and Facilitation

Organizational skills was not mentioned by any of the teacher leaders during the fourth interview. In my opinion, there are a few reasons why this was so. Organization was an important topic in terms of how often it was mentioned in chapter 3 and again in chapter 5. If you recall, chapter 3 examined the results of the second interview that occurred in late October. By this time, many of the teacher leaders mentioned falling into a routine and how important it was to maintain an organized calendar full of events and tasks that needed to be completed during the week and also during that month.

In chapter 5, many of the teacher leaders mention in their answers references to calendars, organization, and the importance of keeping things straight. One teacher leader even joked about how quickly her "free time" disappeared on her calendar. My hypothesis is that by the end of the school year, most teacher leaders had command of this essential skill and it had become so commonplace in their daily routines that it didn't merit much discussion.

Another skill that was conspicuously absent from the final interview responses was facilitation. Some of the teacher leaders mentioned meetings that they attended with their principal or with other teacher leaders in the district, but none mentioned facilitating a meeting with classroom teachers or any other teachers for that matter.

Because this skill was not cited in the final interview did not mean that at least a few of the teacher leaders did not facilitate a meeting. During one of my observation days, I had the pleasure of sitting in on a meeting that was facilitated by two of the teacher leaders who participated in this study. They spoke to the entire teaching staff at their school about the topics of developing quality formative assessments and summative assessments. They both were engaging, organized, asked many questions, and had quality examples that were shared with their colleagues.

All of these components (engaging, organization, use of relevant examples) were mentioned in chapter 2 in relation to facilitation skills. A fifth interview might produce evidence of more examples of facilitation, but the fact that it wasn't mentioned by any of the teacher leaders in this final interview demonstrated that there was little being done during the first year to experience and hone this very essential skill.

REFLECTION

Another teacher leader skill that fell a little short during the final interview was reflection. The importance of keeping a personal journal was mentioned in the introduction, in the chapter 2 summary, and again in the "Recommendations" section of chapter 4. Only one of the five teacher leaders mentioned keeping a weekly journal throughout the study.

In order for reflection to be considered a leadership skill, I would expect reflection or journaling to be mentioned frequently during the final interview. This wasn't the case. Reflection was mentioned, but it was in the context of what the classroom teachers should be doing rather than a skill that was practiced by the teacher leaders. TLA did mention reflection in one of her responses that evaluated how effective she was in her current position. She argued, "Another thing complicating this [her being effective] is that teachers just don't have time to self-reflect and evaluate themselves."

Reflection was mentioned in chapter 5 as well in a comment under the heading "Gain or Loss." Once again, any reference to reflection was in the context of what classroom teachers should be doing rather than a self-reflection of the teacher leader's abilities or progress toward developing this important teacher leadership skill. In order to continue to develop this essential skill, it is recommended that reflective journaling should become a key component in the weekly tasks all new teacher leaders should perform.

RESEARCH

Much like reflection, research was mentioned on a few different occasions during the final interviews. The comments made by the participants were in reference to research that they had performed rather than statements that specifically mentioned or were related to action research as it was described in chapter 2. TLD stated in one of his responses about role change,

> The more I read the studies done about it [teacher leadership] . . . I think we have good instincts with what we have implemented and see some of what we are doing in the research we are reading . . . it would have been nice to have it in reverse, though.

It makes perfect sense that in their first year most teacher leaders would be looking for books or articles specific to teacher leadership. A few of the participants did mention in the "Moving In" stage that they had read as much as they could about teacher leadership in the summer months prior to the beginning of the school year.

At the conclusion of the first year, the scope of their research had narrowed from general information to a more specific examination of particular problem areas that were identified after year one. Later in this chapter, in the segment devoted to recommendations for future teacher leaders, a few of these areas will be examined in greater detail.

It is safe to state that the first-year teacher leaders who participated in this study were a long way from performing true action research as described in chapter 2. This doesn't mean that action research isn't important for all first-year teacher leaders, but it does signify that it was not a focus for our five participants. If it was, at least one of them would have mentioned their working alone or with a group of classroom teachers on selecting a focus for their investigation, the development of research questions, or collecting and analyzing data.

MODELING

One of the biggest surprises at the end of the research was that only one of the five teacher leaders mentioned modeling in their responses. Coquyt and Creasman (2017) give this important skill the attention it deserves by listing how often modeling is mentioned in the Teacher Leader Model Standards.

Domain 1/Function B: Models effective skills in listening, presenting ideas, leading discussions, clarifying, mediating, and identifying the needs of self and others in order to advance shared goals and professional learning.

Domain 2: The teacher leader understands how research creates new knowledge, informs policies and practices, and improves teaching and learning. The teacher leader models and facilitates the use of systematic inquiry as a critical component of teachers' ongoing learning and development.

Domain 4: The teacher leader demonstrates a deep understanding of the teaching and learning processes and uses this knowledge to advance the professional skills of colleagues by being a continuous learner and modeling reflective practice based on student results. The teacher leader works collaboratively with colleagues to ensure instructional practices are aligned to a shared vision, mission, and goals.

Domain 6/Function B: Models and teaches effective communication and collaboration skills with families and other stakeholders focused on attaining equitable achievement for students of all backgrounds and circumstances (pp. 108–10).

TLB did reference modeling in one of her responses, and it was clear that she understands the importance of this skill but did not infer that there were specific situations in which she modeled something for the classroom teachers she was working with. She asserted,

> I have to reiterate that a little bit . . . I have been pulled back into the classroom a little bit more than she has . . . to me one of the exciting things about taking this job was that I thought I could model how I teach . . . if I could show it . . . but the problem is that I am subbing and not modeling. When I am in the classroom

subbing the students are constantly asking me if I am going to come back . . . the kids are appreciative but this isn't the way it is supposed to go . . . the teachers who need to see me modeling aren't in the room. In this sense I don't think I am as effective as I thought I would be in actually helping teachers teach better.

CHAPTER SUMMARY

It is safe to conclude that all of the five teacher leaders showed some improvement in their leadership capacity and also demonstrated elements of growth in many of the leadership skills that were listed at the beginning of this chapter. The idea of servant leadership has been mentioned by some of the participants in a few of my previous research endeavors, but authenticity as a disposition teacher leaders should possess was definitely new to me. Coquyt and Creasman (2017) developed a list of nine dispositions many teacher leaders possess. Following this research, I have taken the liberty of adding authenticity to that list.

1. Innovative/Outside the box thinking
2. Risk taker
3. Growth mindset
4. Passionate
5. Empathetic
6. Respected and/or respect for colleagues
7. Good communicator/listener
8. Quality teaching
9. Initiative
10. Authenticity

Of the ten teacher leader skills that were mentioned at the beginning of this chapter, experience working with adults and having a good working definition of Adult Learning Theory topped the list of skills that were needed the most. Simply having experience working with adults in the past will not be enough for the first-year teacher leader. Coquyt and Creasman (2017) provide a quality definition of Adult Learning Theory and also offer Jim Knight's (2007) partnership philosophy as another quality resource for first-year teacher leaders to read while they prepare for their first year in their new positions (pp. 99–102).

Experience with communication and listening (collaboration) are the next two skills that will benefit the first-year teacher leader. Of course, experience communicating with and collaborating with adults will benefit the first-year teacher leader the most. Those skills that garnered little attention in this research were advocacy, reflection, Big Picture thinking, and organization skills.

The use of the word "garnered" is utilized to indicate that these skills were mentioned by some of the participants, just not at the same degree as the first three. The teacher leadership skills that were not mentioned at all by the participants were modeling, research, and facilitation. This isn't to state unequivocally that these skills will not be utilized in the first year for all teacher leaders, but they were not mentioned by any of the participants in this research.

It seems fitting that the last portion of this chapter provide a list of teacher leadership skills, once again, but this time also include the importance and significance (G = Great, L = Little, N = None) for first-year teacher leaders to research and hone these very important skills during the summer months preceding the beginning of the school year.

- Adult Learning Theory   G
- Communication   G
- Listening/Collaboration   G
- Reflection   L
- Big Picture Thinking/Philosophy   L
- Advocacy   L
- Research (Action Research)   N
- Modeling   N
- Organization   N
- Facilitation   N

Conclusion
Parting Shots

My hope is that the information provided in this and in the preceding chapters serves as a laudable starting point and guide for those venturing into teacher leadership for the first time. The experiences these five novice teacher leaders had while moving in, moving through, and moving out of the first year in their new roles were not all positive and I think that is a good thing. The reader has the benefit of learning from their mistakes and plan accordingly. On the flipside, what worked well should be emulated and modified to meet your specific needs. There is no substitute for experience but the next best thing is reading about the experiences of others. The journey to becoming an effective teacher leader needs to start somewhere, and my parting shot includes four recommendations that will point you in the right direction.

1. Keep a journal of your daily activities and interactions with those that you are working with. This will serve you well not only for your Professional Development Report, but also as a resource to use when you reflect on your weekly interactions and the activities that were valuable and those that could be improved upon.

2. Make certain that nothing you do in your new role, or as you will discover, begin to do because it is needed or right, are associated with the words evaluative, punitive, or coercive. These types of tasks are administrative obligations, not yours.

3. Put the ten teacher leadership skills and dispositions on a wall in your office or room as a constant reminder, a conceptual framework if you will, of what it is that you should be focusing your efforts on each day.

4. Meet with other teacher leaders in your building or in your district on a
   regular basis. Share your successes and challenges with this group and
   agree that no topic is off the table. This is a valuable time for you to vent,
   triumph, or lament about your experiences with those who truly understand what it is that you are going through.

Stay positive, continue to push yourself to learn more about teacher leaders,
and always be a reflective practitioner. Good luck and take care.

—Michael

Appendix A

Four Ss 1–4 represent the interview sequence.	Moving In (MI) Up to 2nd Week	Moving Through (MT) 2nd Week to Holiday Break	Moving Out (MO) End of the School Year
Situation			
New Role	1	3	4
Positive or Negative?	1	3	4
Gradual or Sudden?	1	3	
Internal or External?	1		
Gain or Loss?		3	4
Duration			
Colleagues—Impression	1		
Knowledge of Teacher 　Leadership	1		
Self			
Strengths/Weaknesses		2 and 3	
Control		3	4
Resiliency		3	
Options		3	4
Stage of Life		3	
Previous Experience— 　Adaptability		2	
Support			
Spouse/Partner/Family		2	
Workspace—Physical Setting		2	
Co-Workers	1	2	4
Institutional and Other 　Organizations		2	4

(continued)

Strategies—Coping

Psycho—Self-Esteem/Personal Worth	2	
Optimistic—Hope	2	
Cope Well in Different Settings	2	4
Goal Setting	2	
Planning	2	4
Health	2	
Manage Emotions and Stress	3	4
Change View of Situation/ Flexibility	2	4

Appendix B

Effective School Characteristic No. 1: Clear and Shared Focus

Everybody knows where they are going and why. The focus is on achieving a shared vision, and all understand their role in achieving the vision. The focus and vision are developed from common beliefs and values, creating a consistent direction for all involved.

The Role of an Education Leader	The Role of a Teacher Leader
An education leader <u>develops the capacity</u> for distributed leadership *(ISLLC 2011 3d)*.	*A teacher leader* <u>utilizes group processes</u> to help colleagues work collaboratively to solve problems, make decisions, manage conflict, and promote meaningful change *(TLMS 1a)*.
	A teacher leader <u>serves as a team leader</u> to harness the skills, expertise, and knowledge of colleagues to address curricular expectations and student learning needs *(TLMS 4d)*.
An education leader <u>monitors and evaluates</u> the impact of the instructional program *(ISLLC 2011 2i)*.	*A teacher leader* <u>facilitates the collection, analysis, and use</u> of classroom- and school-based data to identify opportunities to improve curriculum, instruction, assessment, school organization, and school culture *(TLMS 4a)*.

(continued)

The Role of an Education Leader	The Role of a Teacher Leader
An education leader <u>promotes the use</u> of the most effective and appropriate technologies to support teaching and learning *(ISLLC 2011 2h)*.	*A teacher leader* uses knowledge of existing and emerging technologies to <u>guide colleagues</u> to help students skillfully and appropriately navigate the universe of knowledge available on the Internet, use social media to promote collaborative learning, and connect with people and resources around the globe *(TLMS 4e)*.

Effective School Characteristic No. 2:
High Standards and Expectations for All Students

Teachers and staff believe that all students can learn and meet high standards. While recognizing that some students must overcome significant barriers, these obstacles are not seen as insurmountable. Students are offered an ambitious and rigorous course of study.

The Role of An Education Leader	The Role of a Teacher Leader
An education leader <u>collects and analyzes data</u> and information pertinent to the educational environment *(ISLLC 2011 4a)*. *An education leader* <u>monitors and evaluates</u> progress and revises plans *(ISLLC 2011 1e)*.	*A teacher leader* <u>assists colleagues</u> in accessing and using research in order to select appropriate strategies to improve student learning *(TLMS 2a)*. *A teacher leader* <u>facilitates the analysis of student learning data</u>, collaborative interpretation of results, and application of findings to improve teaching and learning *(TLMS 2b)*.
An education leader <u>builds and sustains</u> productive relationships with community partners *(ISLLC 2011 4d)*.	*A teacher leader* <u>uses knowledge and understanding</u> of different backgrounds, ethnicities, cultures, and languages in the school community to promote effective interactions among colleagues, families, and the larger community *(TLMS 6a)*.
An education leader <u>collects and uses data</u> to identify goals, assess organization effectiveness, and promote organizational learning *(ISLLC 2011 1b)*.	*A teacher leader* <u>teaches and supports colleagues to collect, analyze, and communicate data</u> from their classrooms to improve teaching and learning *(TLMS 2d)*.

Effective School Characteristic No. 3: Effective School Leadership

Effective instructional and administrative leadership is required to implement change processes. Effective leaders are proactive and seek help that is needed. They also nurture an instructional program and school culture conducive to learning and professional growth. Effective leaders can have different styles and roles—teachers and other staff, including those in the district office, often have a leadership role.

The Role of an Education Leader	The Role of a Teacher Leader
An education leader collaboratively **develops and implements** a shared vision and mission *(ISLLC 2011 1a)*.	*A teacher leader* **collaborates** with colleagues and school administrators to plan professional learning that is team based, job embedded over time, aligned with content standards, and linked to school/district improvement goals *(TLMS 3a)*.
An education leader **obtains, allocates, aligns, and efficiently utilizes** human, fiscal, and technological resources *(ISLLC 2011 3b)*.	*A teacher leader* **uses information** about adult learning to respond to the diverse learning needs of colleagues by **identifying, promoting, and facilitating** varied and differentiated professional learning *(TLMS 3b)*.
An education leader **promotes the use** of the most effective and appropriate technologies to support teaching and learning *(ISLLC 2011 2h)*.	*A teacher leader* **identifies and uses** appropriate technologies to promote collaborative and differentiated professional learning *(TLMS 3d)*.
An education leader **maximizes time** spent on quality instrution *(ISLLC 2011 2g)*.	*A teacher leader* **advocates** for sufficient preparation, time, and support for colleagues to work in teams to engage in job-embedded professional learning *(TLMS 3f)*.

Effective School Characteristic No. 4: High Levels of Collaboration and Communication

There is strong teamwork among teachers across all grades and with other staff. Everybody is involved and connected to each other, including parents and members of the community, to identify problems and work on solutions.

The Role of an Education Leader	The Role of a Teacher Leader
An education leader **develops** the instructional and leadership capacity of staff *(ISLLC 2011 2f)*.	*A teacher leader* **collaborates** with colleagues and school administrators to plan professional learning that is team based, job embedded, sustained over time, aligned with content standards, and linked to school/district improvement goals *(TLMS 3a)*.

(continued)

The Role of an Education Leader	The Role of a Teacher Leader
An education leader <u>collects and uses data to identify</u> goals, assess organization effectiveness, and promote organizational learning *(ISLLC 2011 1b)*.	*A teacher leader* <u>works with colleagues to collect, analyze, and disseminate data</u> related to the quality of professional learning and its effect on teaching and student learning *(TLMS 3e)*.
An education leader <u>ensures</u> teacher and organizational <u>time is focused</u> to support quality instruction and student learning *(ISLLC 2011 3e)*.	*A teacher leader* <u>engages in reflective dialog</u> with colleagues based on observation of instruction, student work, and assessment data and helps make connections to research-based effective practices *(TLMS 4b)*.
An education leader <u>promotes understanding</u>, appreciation, and use of the community's diverse cultural, social, and intellectual resources *(ISLLC 2011 4b)*.	*A teacher leader* <u>uses knowledge and understanding of different backgrounds, ethnicities, cultures, and languages</u> in the school community to promote effective interactions among colleagues, families, and the larger community *(TLMS 6a)*.

Effective School Characteristic No. 5: Curriculum, Instruction, and Assessments Aligned with State Standards

The planned and actual curricula align with the essential academic learning requirements. Research-based teaching strategies and materials are used. Staff understands the role of classroom and state assessments, what the assessments measure, and how student work is evaluated.

The Role of an Education Leader	The Role of a Teacher Leader
An education leader <u>collects and analyzes data</u> and information pertinent to the educational environment *(ISLLC 2011 4a)*.	*A teacher leader* <u>assists colleagues in accessing and using research</u> in order to select appropriate strategies to improve student learning *(TLMS 2a)*.
An education leader <u>monitors and evaluates</u> the management and operational systems *(ISLLC 2011 3a)*.	*A teacher leader* <u>facilitates the analysis</u> of student learning data, collaborative interpretation of results, and application of findings to improve teaching and learning *(TLMS 2b)*.
An education leader <u>builds and sustains</u> productive relationships with community partners *(ISLLC 2011 4d)*,	*A teacher leader* <u>supports colleagues in collaborating</u> with the higher education institutions and other organizations engaged in researching critical educational issues *(TLMS 2c)*.

The Role of an Education Leader	The Role of a Teacher Leader
An education leader **promotes** continuous and sustainable improvement *(ISLLC 2011 1d)*.	*A teacher leader* **collaborates with colleagues** in the design, implementation, scoring, and interpretation of student data to improve educational practice and student learning *(TLMS 5b)*.

Effective School Characteristic No. 6: Frequent Monitoring of Learning and Teaching

Effective instructional and administrative leadership is required to implement change processes. Effective leaders are proactive and seek help that is needed. They also nurture an instructional program and school culture conducive to learning and professional growth. Effective leaders can have different styles and roles—teachers and other staff, including those in the district office, often have a leadership role.

The Role of an Education Leader	The Role of a Teacher Leader
An education leader **maximizes time spent** on quality instruction *(ISLLC 2011 2g)*.	*A teacher leader* **advocates for** sufficient preparation, time, and support for colleagues to work in teams to engage in job-embedded professional learning *(TLMS 3f)*.
An educational leader **creates** a comprehensive, rigorous, and coherent curricular program *(ISLLC 2011 2b)*.	*A teacher leader* **engages in** reflective dialog with colleagues based on observation of instruction, student work, and assessment data and helps make connections to research-based effective practices *(TLMS 4b)*.
An education leader **develops** assessment and accountability systems to monitor student progress *(ISLLC 2011 2e)*. *An education leader* **ensures** a system of accountability for every student's academic and social success *(ISLLC 2011 5a)*.	*A teacher leader* **collaborates** with colleagues in the design, implementation, scoring, and interpretation of student data to improve educational practice and student learning *(TLMS 5b)*.

Effective School Characteristic No. 7: Focused Professional Development

A strong emphasis is placed on training staff in areas of most need. Feedback from learning and teaching focuses on extensive and ongoing professional development. The support is also aligned with the school or district vision and objectives

The Role of an Education Leader	The Role of a Teacher Leader
An education leader **creates and implements** plans to achieve goals *(ISLLC 2011 1c)*.	*A teacher leader* **utilizes** group processes to help colleagues work collaboratively to solve problems, make decisions, manage conflict, and promote meaningful change *(TLMS 1a)*.

(continued)

The Role of an Education Leader	The Role of a Teacher Leader
An education leader <u>collects and analyzes</u> data and information pertinent to the educational environment *(ISLLC 2011 4a).*	*A teacher leader* <u>assists colleagues</u> in accessing and using research in order to select appropriate strategies to improve student learning *(TLMS 2a).* *A teacher leader* <u>facilitates the analysis</u> of student learning data, collaborative interpretation of results, and application of findings to improve teaching and learning *(TLMS 2b).*
An education leader <u>creates</u> a personalized and motivating learning environment for students *(ISLLC 2011 2c).*	*A teacher leader* <u>serves as a team leader</u> to harness the skills, expertise, and knowledge of colleagues to address curricular expectations and student learning needs *(TLMS 4d).*

Effective School Characteristic No. 8: Supportive Learning Environment

The school has a safe, civil, healthy, and intellectually stimulating learning environment. Students feel respected and connected with the staff and are engaged in learning. Instruction is personalized and small learning environments increase student contact with teachers.

The Role of an Education Leader	The Role of a Teacher Leader
An education leader <u>safeguards</u> the values of democracy, equity, and diversity *(ISLLC 2011 5c).*	*A teacher leader* <u>facilitates</u> colleagues' self-examination of their understandings of community culture and diversity and how they can develop culturally responsive strategies to enrich the educational experiences of students and achieve high levels of learning for all students *(TLMS 6c).*
An education leader <u>builds and sustains</u> positive relationships with families and caregivers *(ISLLC 2011 4c).*	*A teacher leader* <u>develops a shared understanding</u> among colleagues of the diverse educational needs of families and the community *(TLMS 6d).* *A teacher leader* <u>collaborates</u> with families, communities, and colleagues to develop comprehensive strategies to address the diverse educational needs of families and the community *(TLMS 6e).*

The Role of an Education Leader	The Role of a Teacher Leader
An education leader **considers and evaluates** the potential moral and legal consequences of decision making *(ISLLC 2011 5d)*. *An education leader* **promotes** social justice and ensures that individual student needs inform all aspects of schooling *(ISLLC 2011 5e)*.	*A teacher leader* **collaborates** with colleagues to select appropriate opportunities to advocate for the rights and/or needs of students, to secure additional resources within the building or district that support student learning, and to communicate effectively with targeted audiences such as parents and community members *(TLMS 7c)*.

Effective School Characteristic No. 9:
High Level of Family and Community Involvement

There is a sense that all have a responsibility to educate students, not just the teachers and staff in schools. Families as well as businesses, social service agencies, and community colleges/universities all play a vital role in this effort.

The Role of an Education Leader	The Role of a Teacher Leader
An education leader **builds and sustains** productive relationships with community partners *(ISLLC 2011 4d)*.	*A teacher leader* **uses knowledge and understanding** of the different backgrounds, ethnicities, cultures, and languages in the school community to promote effective interactions among colleagues, families, and the larger community *(TLMS 6a)*.
An education leader **promotes** understanding, appreciation, and use of the community's diverse cultural, social, and intellectual resources *(ISLLC 2011 4b)*.	*A teacher leader* **models and teaches** effective communication and collaboration skills with families and other stakeholders focused on attaining equitable achievement for students of all backgrounds and circumstances *(TLMS 6b)*.
An education leader **safeguards** the values of democracy, equity, and diversity *(ISLLC 2011 5c)*.	*A teacher leader* **facilitates colleagues' self-examination** of their own understandings of community culture and diversity and how they can develop culturally responsive strategies to enrich the educational experiences of students and achieve high levels of learning for all students *(TLMS 6c)*.

Appendix C

Date/Day	Time	Activity	Purpose
Sept. 5/ Tuesday	8:00	Meeting with Vice Principal Boone to discuss first semester professional development schedule.	• Identification of activities or presentations to assist, promote, support, and lead. • Share **goals** and amend if need be.
	9:00	Meet with Ms. Kalhoff to explain to her what my role is for this year.	• Ms. Kalhoff is a seasoned veteran in the English department. It seems that some of the teachers have been asking exactly what it is that I will be doing this year. • Ideal opportunity for me to explain how my role is to be more of a facilitator rather than evaluator. • Opportunity to explain the differences between what I will be doing versus what administration does.
	10:00	Read chapters 1 and 2 in *The Leader Within*.	• Become more familiar with Domains 1 and 2 in the Teacher Leader Model Standards. • Perform various self-reflection activities offered throughout the chapters and take notes in reflective journal. • Become more informed about how to impact school culture and the use of research in my position.

(continued)

Date/Day	Time	Activity	Purpose
	11:30	Lunch with colleague and fellow teacher leader (Jill Bakus).	• Go over tentative schedule for the two of us to meet throughout the week (Tuesday and Thursday at 3:30) to share our experiences, successes, and challenges as we journey through this new experience together.

Appendix D

MODEL TEACHER LEADER STANDARDS

The Standards, Domain 1:
Fostering a Collaborative Culture to Support Educator Development and Student Learning

The teacher leader is well versed in adult learning theory and uses that knowledge to create a community of collective responsibility within his or her school. In promoting this collaborative culture among fellow teachers, administrators, and other school leaders, the teacher leader ensures improvement in educator instruction and, consequently, student learning.

Functions

The teacher leader

a) utilizes group processes to help colleagues work collaboratively to solve problems, make decisions, manage conflict, and promote meaningful change;
b) **models effective skills** in listening, presenting ideas, leading discussions, clarifying, mediating, and identifying the needs of self and others in order to advance shared goals and professional learning;
c) **employs facilitation skills** to create trust among colleagues, develop collective wisdom, and build ownership and action that supports student learning;
d) strives to create an inclusive culture in which diverse perspectives are welcomed in addressing challenges; and
e) **uses knowledge and understanding of different backgrounds, ethnicities, cultures, and languages** to promote effective interactions among colleagues.

The Standards, Domain 2:
Accessing and Using Research to Improve Practice and Student Learning

The teacher leader keeps abreast of the latest research about teaching effectiveness and student learning and implements best practices where appropriate. He or she models the use of systematic inquiry as a critical component of teachers' ongoing learning and development.

Functions

The teacher leader

a) assists colleagues in accessing and using research in order to select appropriate strategies to improve student learning;
b) facilitates the analysis of student learning data, collaborative interpretation of results, and application of findings to improve teaching and learning;
c) supports colleagues in collaborating with the higher education institutions and other organizations engaged in researching critical educational issues; and
d) teaches and supports colleagues to collect, analyze, and communicate data from their classrooms to improve teaching and learning.

The Standards, Domain 3:
Promoting Professional Learning for Continuous Improvement

The teacher leader understands that the processes of teaching and learning are constantly evolving. The teacher leader designs and facilitates job-embedded professional development opportunities that are aligned with school improvement goals.

Functions

The teacher leader

a) collaborates with colleagues and school administrators to plan professional learning that is team based, job embedded, sustained over time, aligned with content standards, and linked to school/district improvement goals;
b) uses information about adult learning to respond to the diverse learning needs of colleagues by identifying, promoting, and facilitating varied and differentiated professional learning;
c) facilitates professional learning among colleagues;
d) identifies and uses appropriate technologies to promote collaborative and differentiated professional learning;

e) works with colleagues to collect, analyze, and disseminate data related to the quality of professional learning and its effect on teaching and student learning;

f) advocates for sufficient preparation, time, and support for colleagues to work in teams to engage in job-embedded professional learning;

g) provides constructive feedback to colleagues to strengthen teaching practice and improve student learning; and

h) uses information about emerging education, economic, and social trends in planning and facilitating professional learning.

The Standards, Domain 4: Facilitating Improvements in Instruction and Student Learning

The teacher leader possesses a deep understanding of teaching and learning and models an attitude of continuous learning and reflective practice for colleagues. The teacher leader works collaboratively with fellow teachers to constantly improve instructional practices.

Functions

The teacher leader

a) facilitates the collection, analysis, and use of classroom- and school-based data to identify opportunities to improve curriculum, instruction, assessment, school organization, and school culture;

b) engages in reflective dialog with colleagues based on observation of instruction, student work, and assessment data and helps make connections to research-based effective practices;

c) supports colleagues' individual and collective reflection and professional growth by serving in roles such as mentor, coach, and content facilitator;

d) serves as a team leader to harness the skills, expertise, and knowledge of colleagues to address curricular expectations and student learning needs;

e) uses knowledge of existing and emerging technologies to guide colleagues in helping students skillfully and appropriately navigate the universe of knowledge available on the Internet, use social media to promote collaborative learning, and connect with people and resources around the globe; and

f) promotes instructional strategies that address issues of diversity and equity in the classroom and ensures that individual student learning needs remain the central focus of instruction.

The Standards, Domain 5:
Promoting the Use of Assessments and Data for School and District Improvement

The teacher leader is knowledgeable about the design of assessments, both formative and summative. He or she works with colleagues to analyze data and interpret results to inform goals and to improve student learning.

Functions

The teacher leader

a) increases the capacity of colleagues to identify and use multiple assessment tools aligned to state and local standards;
b) collaborates with colleagues in the design, implementation, scoring, and interpretation of student data to improve educational practice and student learning;
c) creates a climate of trust and critical reflection in order to engage colleagues in challenging conversations about student learning data that lead to solutions to identified issues; and
d) works with colleagues to use assessment and data findings to promote changes in instructional practices or organizational structures to improve student learning.

The Standards, Domain 6:
Improving Outreach and Collaboration with Families and Community

The teacher leader understands the impact that families, cultures, and communities have on student learning. As a result, the teacher leader seeks to promote a sense of partnership among these different groups toward the common goal of excellent education.

Functions

The teacher leader

a) uses knowledge and understanding of the different backgrounds, ethnicities, cultures, and languages in the school community to promote effective interactions among colleagues, families, and the larger community;
b) models and teaches effective communication and collaboration skills with families and other stakeholders focused on attaining equitable achievement for students of all backgrounds and circumstances;

c) facilitates colleagues' self-examination of their own understandings of community culture and diversity and how they can develop culturally responsive strategies to enrich the educational experiences of students and achieve high levels of learning for all students;
d) develops a shared understanding among colleagues of the diverse educational needs of families and the community; and
e) collaborates with families, communities, and colleagues to develop comprehensive strategies to address the diverse educational needs of families and the community.

The Standards, Domain 7:
Advocating for Student Learning and the Profession

The teacher leader understands the landscape of education policy and can identify key players at the local, state, and national levels. The teacher leader advocates for the teaching profession and for policies that benefit student learning.

Functions

The teacher leader

a) shares information with colleagues within and/or beyond the district regarding how local, state, and national trends and policies can impact classroom practices and expectations for student learning;
b) works with colleagues to identify and use research to advocate for teaching and learning processes that meet the needs of all students;
c) collaborates with colleagues to select appropriate opportunities to advocate for the rights and/or needs of students, to secure additional resources within the building or district that support student learning, and to communicate effectively with targeted audiences such as parents and community members;
d) advocates for access to professional resources, including financial support and human and other material resources, that allow colleagues to spend significant time learning about effective practices and developing a professional learning community focused on school improvement goals; and
e) represents and advocates for the profession in contexts outside the classroom.

Bibliography

PREFACE

Schlossberg, N. K. (1981). A model for analyzing human adaptation to transition. *The Counseling Psychologist, 9*(2), 2–18.

INTRODUCTION

Schlossberg, N. K. (1981). A model for analyzing human adaptation to transition. *The Counseling Psychologist, 9*(2), 2–18.

Struyve, C., Meredith, C., & Gielen, S. (2014). Who am I and where do I belong? The perception and evaluation of teacher leaders concerning teacher leadership practices and micropolitics in schools. *Journal of Educational Change, 15*(2), 701–718.

CHAPTER 1

Allio, R., (2005). Leadership development: Teaching versus learning. *Management Decision, 43*(7/8), 1071–1077.

Badarocco, J. L. Jr (2002). Leading quietly: An unorthodox guide to doing the right thing. Boston, MA: Harvard Business School Press.

Chickering, A. W., & Schlossberg, N. K. (1995). *Getting the most out of college.* Needham Heights, MA: Allyn and Bacon.

Creasman, B., & Coquyt, M. (2016). *The leader within: Understanding and empowering teacher leaders*. Lanham, MD: Rowman & Littlefield.

Collins, J. (2001). "Level 5 leadership", *Harvard Business Review* (January), 79, 67–76.

Coquyt, M., & Creasman, B. (2017). *Growing leaders within: A process toward teacher leadership*. Lanham, MD: Rowman & Littlefield.

Crowther, F., Kaagan, S., Ferguson, M., & Hann, L. (2002). *Developing teacher leaders: How teacher leadership enhances school success*. Thousand Oaks, CA: Corwin Press.

Evans, N. J., Forney, D. S., & Guido-DiBrito, F. (1998). *Student development in college theory, research, and practice*. San Francisco, CA: Jossey-Bass.

Evans, N. J., Forney, D. S., Guido, F., Patton, L. D., & Renn, K. A. (2010). Schlossberg's transition theory. In D. Brightman & E. Null (Eds.), *Student development in college: Theory, research and practice* (2nd ed.; pp. 212–226) San Francisco, CA: Jossey-Bass.

Goodman, J., Schlossberg, N. K., & Anderson, M. L. (2006). *Counseling adults in transition: Linking practice with theory* (3rd ed.). New York: Springer.

Komives, S. R., & Brown, S. C. (n.d.). *A facilitator guide for seniors: Four years in retrospect*. Retrieved on April 28, 2008. http://www.newsreel.org/guides/seniorsg.htm.

Kouzes, J., & Posner, B. (2002). *The leadership challenge*. San Francisco, CA: Jossey-Bass.

Mangin, M. M., & Stoelinga, S. R. (Eds.). (2008). *Effective teacher leadership: Using research to inform practice*. New York: Teachers College Press.

Muijs, D., & Harris, A. (2006). Teacher led school improvement: Teacher leadership in the UK. *Teaching and Teacher Education, 22*(8), 961–972. http://dx.doi.org/10.1016/j.tate.2006.04.010.

Muijs, D., & Harris, A. (2007). Teacher Leadership in (in)action: Three case studies of contrasting schools. *Educational Management Administration & Leadership, 35*(1), 111–134.

Neumerski, C. M. (2012). Rethinking instructional leadership, a review: What do we know about principal, teacher, and coach instructional leadership, and where should we go from here? *Educational Administration Quarterly, 49*(2), 310–347.

Rosenholtz, S. (1989). *Teachers' workplace: The social organization of schools*. New York: Longmans.

Sargent, A. G., & Schlossberg, N. K. (1988). Managing adult transitions. *Training & Development Journal, 42*(12), 58–60.

Schlossberg, N. K. (1981). A model for analyzing human adaptation to transition. *The Counseling Psychologist, 9*(2), 2–18.

Schlossberg, N. K., Waters, E. B., & Goodman, J. (1995). *Counseling adults in transition: Linking practice with theory* (2nd ed.). New York: Springer.

Smylie, M. A. (1995). New perspectives on teacher leadership. *The Elementary School Journal, 96*(1), 3–7.

Smylie, M. A. (1997). Research on teacher leadership: Assessing the state of the art. In B. J. Biddle, T. L. Good, & I. F. Goodson (Eds.), *International handbook of teachers and teaching* (pp. 521–592). Dordrecht: Kluwer Academic Publishers.

Struyve, C., Meredith, C., & Gielen, S. (2014). Who am I and where do I belong? The perception and evaluation of teacher leaders concerning teacher leadership practices and micropolitics in schools. *Journal of Educational Change, 15*(2), 701–18.

Teacher Leadership Exploratory Consortium. (2012). Teacher leader model standards. Retrieved from http://www.teacherleaderstandards.org.

Wenner, J. A., & Campbell, T. (2016). The theoretical and empirical basis of teacher leadership: A review of the literature. *Review of Educational Research, 87*(1), 134–171.

Wilson, M. (1993). The search for teacher leaders. *Educational Leadership, 50*(6), 24–27.

York-Barr, J., & Duke, K. (2004). What do we know about teacher leadership? Findings from two decades of scholarship. *Review of Educational Research, 74*(3), 255–316.

CHAPTER 2

Ash, R., & Persall, M. (2000) The principal as chief learning officer: Developing teacher leaders. *NASSP Bulletin, 84*(616): 15–22.

Barth, R. S. (2013). The time is ripe (again). *Educational Leadership, 71*(2), 10–16. Retrieved from http://www.ascd.org/publications/educational-leadership/oct13/vol71/num02/The-Time-Is-Ripe-%28Again%29.aspx.

Coquyt, M., & Creasman, B. (2017). *Growing leaders within: A process toward teacher leadership.* Lanham, MD: Rowman & Littlefield.

Cuthbertson, J. (2014). How to become a teacher advocate. *Education Week Teacher*, November 25. Retrieved from http://www.edweek.org/tm/articles/2014/11/25/ctq-cuthbertson-teacer-advocate.html.

Dewey, J. (1933). *How we think.* New York: Prometheus Books

Gehrke, N. (1991). Developing teacher leadership skills. *ERIC.* Retrieved ED330691 from www.askeric.org.

Harris, A., and Muijs, D. (2003). Teacher leadership: A review of research [electronic version]. *University of Warwick.* Retrieved January 22, 2017 from http://forms.ncsl.org.uk/mediastore/image2/randd-teacher-leadership-full.pdf.

Knapp, M. C. (2017). An autoethnography of a (reluctant) teacher leader. *Journal of Mathematical Behavior, 46*, 251–66.

Lambert, L. (2002). A framework for shared leadership. *Educational Leadership, 59*(8), 37–40.

Muijs, D., & Harris, A. (2003). Teacher leadership and school improvement. *Education Review, 16*(2): 39–42.

Rosenholtz, S. (1989). *Teachers' workplace: The social organization of schools.* New York: Longmans.

Sagor, R. (2000). *Guiding school improvement with action research.* Alexandria, VA: ASCD.

Schlossberg, N. K. (1981). A model for analyzing human adaptation to transition. *The Counseling Psychologist, 9*(2), 2–18.

CHAPTER 3

Coquyt, M., & Creasman, B. (2017). *Growing leaders within: A process toward teacher leadership*. Lanham, MD: Rowman & Littlefield.

Schlossberg, N. K. (1981). A model for analyzing human adaptation to transition. *The Counseling Psychologist, 9*(2), 2–18.

Whitaker, T. (2012). *Shifting the monkey*. Bloomington, IN: Triple Nickel Press.

CHAPTER 4

Schlossberg, N. K. (1981). A model for analyzing human adaptation to transition. *The Counseling Psychologist, 9*(2), 2–18.

CHAPTER 5

Chase, M. A. (2010). Should coaches believe in innate ability? The importance of leadership mindset. *Quest, 62*, 296–307.

Dweck, C. S. (2006). *Mindset: The new psychology of success*. New York: Random House.

Johnson, R. (2018, April 18). *On courage and choices: Quotes by well-known self-help authors*. Retrieved from http://www.mindingtherapy.com/on-courage-and-choices/.

Kolb, A. Y., and Kolb, D. A. (2005). Learning styles and learning spaces: Enhancing experiential learning in higher education. *Academy of Management Learning and Education, 4*(2): 193–212.

Kolb, D. A. (1984). *Experiential learning: Experience as the source of learning and development* (Vol. 1). Englewood Cliffs, NJ: Prentice-Hall.

Peck, M. S. (1978). *The road less traveled: A new psychology of love, traditional values and spiritual growth*. New York: Simon and Schuster.

CHAPTER 6

Coquyt, M., & Creasman, B. (2017). *Growing leaders within: A process toward teacher leadership*. Lanham, MD: Rowman & Littlefield.

Knight, J. (2007). *Instructional coaching*. Thousand Oaks, CA: Corwin Press.

About the Author

Michael Coquyt, EdD, is currently an associate professor of education at Minnesota State University Moorhead. He teaches primarily in the educational leadership graduate and doctoral programs. Coquyt also coordinates the curriculum and instruction graduate program. He has served as a superintendent, high school principal, and high school teacher.